KT-407-764

B100 000001 3832 9B

ice cream
and frozen desserts

ice cream
and frozen desserts

Peggy Fallon

LONDON, NEW YORK, MELBOURNE, MUNICH, DELHI

This book is dedicated to JMG—always in my heart.

Editor Nichole Morford
Designer Bill Miller
Managing Art Editor Michelle Baxter
Art Director Dirk Kaufman
Executive Managing Editor Sharon Lucas
Publishing Director Carl Raymond
DTP Coordinator Kathy Farias
Production Manager Ivor Parker
Anglicisation Editor Lee Faber
Editorial Assistant Nicole Turney

Packaged by King Hill Productions
Food Stylist Alison Attenborough
Food photography by Ngoc Minh Ngo, unless noted below:
Author photo by Larry Guyer
Additional ingredient photography by Bill Miller (pages 29, 59, 77, 95, 97)

Published by DK Publishing, 375 Hudson Street, New York, NY 10014
Published in Great Britain in 2007 by Dorling Kindersley Limited,
80 Strand, London WC2R 0RL

Penguin Group (UK)

07 08 09 10 10 9 8 7 6 5 4 3 2 1

Copyright © 2007 by DK Publishing
Text copyright © 2007 by King Hill Productions

All rights reserved. No part of this publication may be reproduced, stored in
a retrieval system, or transmitted in any form or by any means, electronic,
mechanical, photocopying, recording, or otherwise without the prior written
permission of the copyright owners.

A CIP catalogue record for this book is available from the British Library.
ISBN 978-1-4053-2214-0

Reproduced by Colourscan (Singapore)
Printed and bound in China by Leo Paper

Discover more at
www.dk.com

WOLVERHAMPTON LIBRARIES		
B10000000138329B		
HJ	8|67	558658
641.862 FAL		£12.99
TR		ᴋⱳ

Contents

Making Ice Cream at Home

What is America's hands-down absolutely all-time favourite dessert? Ice cream, of course. That pleasing jolt of sweet cold in the mouth, followed by the sensual richness of frozen cream and burst of flavour on the tongue, satisfies in a way few other desserts can. Sometimes there's the added delight of a crackle of nuts or chocolate bits or specks of sweets. Perhaps a whiff of ethereal cream on top, a splash of a liqueur, or the warm, sticky goodness of hot fudge sauce or warm toffee to transform the perfect dessert into an over-the-top sundae.

Of course, ice cream can be purchased almost anywhere, but there's a new twist in the frozen world of desserts: home-made. A generation of improved ice cream makers, freed from salt and ice, many of them with built-in compressors for convenient freezing, has made home-made ice cream making easier—and quicker—than ever.

Controlling the ingredients you feed to your family and involving children in the kitchen are just a couple of good reasons for making ice cream at home. Customising your own flavours and controlling the fat content and level of sweetness are several more. Home-made also allows you to pick from a wide range of types of frozen desserts from creamy to low-fat: rich ice creams, light ice creams, frozen yoghurts, ice milk, gelato, sorbet, sherbets, and granita. Most of all, ice cream making is easy, and it's fun.

In this collection you'll find a range of flavours, from Almost-Instant Banana, Cinnamon-Basil, and Chocolate-Chilli Ice Cream and Espresso Bean Gelato with Toffee Bits to Mango-Pineapple, Pomegranate Martini, and Green Apple Sorbet. Plus, there are over two dozen ideas for "almost instant" recipes—sumptuous desserts quickly assembled from store-bought ingredients. There are recipes for sauces, toppings, and swirls as well.

Ice cream also serves here as a ready-made base for any number of pies, cakes, and creative confections for entertaining. Frozen desserts take an enormous burden off the cook, because they must be prepared in advance. Name a child who wouldn't be delighted by a Chocolate Cookie Ice Cream Cake for her birthday? Or an adult whose eyes wouldn't light up at a Mile-High Lemon Chiffon Ice Cream Pie? Some of these fantasy creations are whimsical. Watermelon Bombe, which looks just like a big slice of fruit, Ice Cream "Jacket Potato," and Spaghetti Ice Cream are guaranteed to be the life of the party.

When making ice cream at home, there are several facts you should know. For one thing, unless you are using a professional machine that costs thousands of pounds, or an old-fashioned salt-and-ice bucket, no home ice cream maker freezes ice cream solid.

Whether you are using a completely automatic machine or an ice cream maker that requires pre-freezing the canister overnight, the end product will be the same: a cohesive mass that is not solid. You could think of it as "soft serve." To transform this semi-frozen product into a proper frozen dessert, the ice cream that comes out of the machine must be transferred to a covered container and set in the freezer for several hours. This final freezing period improves texture and also allows the ice cream to cure and mellow, deepening its flavour.

About Ice Cream Makers

These days, there is an ice cream machine for every budget and every lifestyle. The purpose of any ice cream maker is to break up ice crystals as they form during the freezing process. This constant movement, called churning, also incorporates air to improve the texture and increase the volume of the finished ice cream. Since all types of machines make remarkably good ice cream, you must make your decision based upon convenience, capacity, and budget. As with many things in life, price is often an indicator of quality.

Automatic Ice Cream Machines with Built-In Compressors

Since the introduction of the Simac ice cream machine in the 1980's, the gelato-loving Italians have led the technology revolution. Models like Musso's *Lussino* and *Pola* operate like little Ferraris, though their price tags may make them out of reach for anyone other than the most serious ice cream maker. These models are not stocked in the UK but can be ordered directly from Italy.

Machines made by Gaggia, Magimix, and Cuisinart also have fairly prohibitive price tags, but they make brilliant ice cream. These machines are heavy and take up a lot of room, so unless you plan on using them often, you might want to think about other ice cream machine options.

Frozen-Canister Ice Cream Makers

Brands such as Magimix, Kenwood, Rival, and Phillips all make ice cream machines based around a coolant-filled canister that needs to be frozen until solid and will make around 750ml–1½ litres of ice cream in about 45 minutes. Even KitchenAid makes a special freezer-ready bowl and dasher attachment that converts their stand mixer into an ice cream maker with surprisingly good results. In order for any of these machines to work properly, the bulky canister must be kept in your freezer for a full 24 hours before using, but the advantages are that these machines are lightweight and the cost is quite reasonable.

Novelty Ice Cream Makers

There are also several unconventional methods of making ice cream—involving ziplock bags, empty reclosable food cans and hollow plastic balls. These always require ice and salt. They work after a fashion and may be fun if you're on a camping trip with no electricity available and have an enormous craving for ice cream, but they require a lot of muscle for a very cold, slushy product that hardly resembles ice cream. Try them once as a science experiment with your children, then save your money and buy an ice cream maker.

Ingredient Guide

As with all good food, ingredients are everything in ice cream and other frozen desserts. Your dairy products and eggs should be pristinely fresh, organic if possible. This guide will direct you to the best ice cream making ingredients available.

Chocolate: As a general rule, the higher the cacao content of chocolate, the greater the intensity of flavour. That's because cacao is pure chocolate. Plain dark chocolate must contain a minimum of 35 per cent cacao; many premium brands contain as much as 72 per cent. Sugar is added for sweetness and cocoa butter for smoothness, along with a small amount of vanilla flavouring and soya lecithin as an emulsifier. Many of the better brands now list cacao content on their labels as a sign of quality, though the exact sweetness and bitterness of the finished chocolate is determined by the manufacturer. Unless a certain type of chocolate is specified in the recipe, all plain dark chocolates can be used interchangeably, according to your taste preference. All chocolate should be melted over a very low heat, stirring frequently.

Cocoa powder: Almost all the recipes in this book specify unsweetened cocoa powder. Do not substitute drinking chocolate.

Eggs: Use Large eggs, preferably organic, whenever whole eggs or egg yolks are called for. Slightly larger eggs will not adversely affect the finished product; they'll just add a bit of extra richness. Very Large eggs, however, may throw off the formulas. When an ice cream calls for an egg custard base, you'll note it is cooked to 75–80°C. This ensures all bacteria are killed and thickens the yolks to the proper body needed for a silky, rich frozen cream. Do not let the temperature rise above 80 degrees or the egg yolks may curdle.

Flavour extracts: These must be pure, especially **vanilla**. Otherwise your ice cream will taste artificial and will lack the bright, clean taste of a natural product. **Liqueurs and spirits** are also used as flavourings, especially in sorbets. Since alcohol will never completely freeze, this addition also prevents the sorbet from freezing into a solid mass. Never double or triple the specified amount of alcohol: you'll end up with slush.

Fresh fruits: Fruits and berries should be perfectly ripe. Freezing dulls flavours, so to ensure the essence of a fruit shines through, use produce whose taste and aroma is at its peak.

Double cream: This is cream with a minimum butterfat content of 48 per cent. Whipping cream is a lighter version with a minimum of 35 per cent fat. Double cream and whipping cream can be used interchangeably. If possible, avoid cream labeled "UHT" or "long life."

Milk: Use full cream milk, unless otherwise specified. In most cases, semi skimmed or skimmed milk will result in a frozen dessert that is too icy and will melt too quickly.

Nuts: As most bakers know, nuts are rich in oils that can quickly turn rancid, especially in warm weather. Buy your nuts in a sealed container or in bulk from a good source. Store them in a covered jar or sealed container in the refrigerator or freezer.

Plain yoghurt: Plain means unflavoured. Unless a recipe specifies to use low-fat, be sure to use a full cream milk-based yoghurt.

Salt: A pinch of salt brightens sweet flavours, especially when chocolate is involved.

Sugar: Use pure cane granulated sugar. In addition to its obvious role as a sweetener, sugar plays an important part in determining the texture of finished ice cream. Artificial sweeteners do not react the same; they produce an unpleasantly hard ice cream, which could possibly damage your machine.

Now that you've got the whole scoop, it's time to get started!

"without ice cream, there would be darkness and chaos."

–Don Kardong, 1976 US Olympic marathoner

rich ice creams, frozen custards, & gelatos

Tahitian Double Vanilla Ice Cream

If you love vanilla, why bother with an ice cream recipe that contains only a miserly teaspoon of the luscious essence? This version flaunts a double dose of fragrant vanilla, placing it right at the head of its class. Tahitian vanilla has a heady floral flavour, worth its extra price.

1 Using the pointed tip of a sharp knife, split the vanilla pod in half lengthways and scrape the tiny black seeds into a heavy medium saucepan. Add the vanilla pod, cream, and milk and bring to the simmer over a medium heat. Remove from the heat, cover, and let stand at room temperature for 30 minutes to blend the flavours.

2 Add the sugar and salt. Return to medium heat and cook, stirring occasionally, until the sugar dissolves and the mixture is hot, about 5 minutes.

3 Whisk the egg yolks lightly in a medium bowl. Gradually whisk in about 240ml (8fl oz) of the warm vanilla cream. Return the egg mixture to the saucepan, reduce the heat to medium-low, and cook, stirring, until the custard thickens enough to coat the back of a spoon, 75–80°C. Do not let boil, or the egg yolks will curdle.

4 Sieve the custard into a bowl, pressing through as many of the vanilla seeds as you can. Cover and refrigerate until the custard is very cold, at least 6 hours or as long as 2 days. Stir in the vanilla extract.

5 Pour the custard into the canister of an ice cream maker and freeze according to the manufacturer's directions. Transfer the ice cream to a covered container and freeze until it is firm enough to scoop, at least 3 hours or overnight.

INGREDIENTS

1 vanilla pod, preferably Tahitian
720ml (1½ pints) double cream
240ml (8fl oz) milk
175g (6oz) sugar
Pinch of salt
4 egg yolks
1tbsp Tahitian vanilla extract

Makes about 1 litre (2 pints)

Pistachio Gelato

Pistachio is an old-fashioned flavour that's been embraced by contemporary cuisine. Be sure to choose nuts that are fresh and have not been salted. Just a couple of drops of food colouring impart the familiar pale green of the nuts.

1 In a food processor, combine the pistachios with 4tbsp of the sugar. Pulse until the nuts are finely chopped; take care not to process to a paste.

2 In a heavy medium saucepan, combine the chopped pistachios and the milk. Bring to the simmer over a medium heat. Remove from the heat, cover, and let steep at room temperature for 30 minutes to allow the flavour to develop.

3 Stir in the remaining 115g (4oz) sugar and the salt. Return to medium heat and cook, stirring occasionally, until the sugar dissolves and the mixture is hot, about 5 minutes.

4 Whisk the egg yolks lightly in a medium bowl. Gradually whisk in about 240ml (8fl oz) of the warm pistachio milk. Whisk the egg mixture into the remaining pistachio milk in the saucepan, reduce the heat to medium-low, and cook, stirring, until the custard thickens enough to coat the back of a spoon, 75–80°C. Do not let boil, or the egg yolks will curdle.

5 Sieve the custard into a bowl; discard the nuts. Whisk in the food colouring. Cover and refrigerate for 4 hours, or until the custard is very cold. Stir in the almond extract.

6 Pour the custard into the canister of an ice cream maker and freeze according to the manufacturer's directions. Transfer the gelato to a covered container and freeze until it is firm enough to scoop, at least 3 hours or overnight.

INGREDIENTS

115g (4oz) unsalted shelled pistachio nuts

175g (6oz) sugar

500ml (16fl oz) milk

Pinch of salt

5 egg yolks

2 drops of green food colouring

1tsp almond extract

Makes about 1 litre (2 pints)

COOL TIPS FOR SUCCESS

Use a sugar thermometer or instant-read thermometer to measure the exact temperature of your cooked custard. At 75–80°C, the mixture will be thick enough to coat a spoon and will freeze into a silky, smooth ice cream.

Fresh Peach Ice Cream

Nothing speaks of high summer more than fresh ripe peaches, and this ice cream offers a great way to use them. To peel peaches, slip them into a pot of boiling water for 15–20 seconds, then rinse under cold water. The skins will slip right off.

1 In a food processor, pulse the peaches to chop them coarsely. Add 4tbsp of the sugar and the lemon juice and pulse 2 or 3 times to mix. Do not overprocess to a purée. Transfer to a bowl and let macerate at room temperature for 1 hour.

2 In a heavy medium saucepan, combine the cream and milk. Bring to the simmer over a medium heat. Stir in the remaining 115g (4oz) sugar and the salt and cook, stirring occasionally, until the sugar dissolves and the mixture is hot, about 5 minutes.

3 Whisk the egg yolks lightly in a medium bowl. Gradually whisk in about 240ml (8fl oz) of the warm cream. Return the egg mixture to the saucepan, reduce the heat to medium-low, and cook, stirring, until the custard thickens enough to coat the back of a spoon, 75–80°C. Do not let boil, or the egg yolks will curdle.

4 Sieve the custard into a bowl and stir in the chopped peaches with all their juices. Cover and refrigerate until the custard is very cold, at least 6 hours or as long as 2 days. Stir in the almond extract.

5 Pour the custard into the canister of an ice cream maker and freeze according to the manufacturer's directions. Transfer the ice cream to a covered container and freeze until it is firm enough to scoop, at least 3 hours or overnight.

INGREDIENTS

450g (1lb) ripe peaches, peeled and stoned
175g (6oz) sugar
½tsp fresh lemon juice
720ml (1¼ pints) double cream
240ml (8fl oz) milk
Pinch of salt
4 egg yolks
1tsp almond extract or vanilla extract

Makes about 1 litre (2 pints)

Lemon and Mascarpone Ice Cream

The acidity of the lemons in this ice cream complement the creamy flavour of mascarpone cheese. To cut the tartness of the lemon, dilute with 3tbsp tangerine or orange juice.

1 Preheat the oven to 160°C (325°F/Gas 3). Spread out the almonds on a small baking sheet. Toast in the oven for 7–10 minutes, until the nuts are fragrant and golden. Let cool slightly, then coarsely chop.

2 Grate the rind from 2 of the lemons into a small bowl. Squeeze enough lemons into the bowl to yield 75ml (2½fl oz) lemon juice. Add to the rind with the tangerine or orange juice.

3 In a heavy nonreactive medium saucepan, warm the cream and milk over a medium heat until tiny bubbles form around the edges of the pan. Remove from the heat.

4 Whisk the egg yolks lightly. Gradually whisk in the sugar and beat until well-blended and pale yellow. Gradually whisk in about 240ml (8fl oz) of the warm cream. Slowly whisk the egg yolk mixture into the remaining cream in the saucepan. Cook over medium-low heat, stirring, until the custard thickens enough to coat the back of a spoon, 75–80°C. Do not let boil, or the egg yolks will curdle.

5 Sieve the custard through a fine sieve into a bowl. Let cool for 10 minutes. Whisk in the mascarpone cheese until well-blended. Mix in the lemon rind with the lemon and tangerine or orange juice and the vanilla extract. Cover and refrigerate for at least 3 hours.

6 Pour the lemon custard into the canister of an ice cream maker and freeze according to the manufacturer's directions. Add the chopped toasted almonds and process for 1 minute longer. Transfer the ice cream to a covered container and freeze until it is firm enough to scoop, at least 3 hours or overnight.

INGREDIENTS

45g (1½oz) flaked almonds
4 large lemons
3tbsp tangerine or orange juice
240ml (8fl oz) double cream
240ml (8fl oz) milk
4 egg yolks
175g (6oz) sugar
225g (8oz) mascarpone cheese
1tsp vanilla extract

Makes about 1 litre (2 pints)

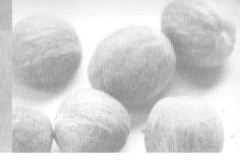

Lemon-Nutmeg
Frozen Custard

What looks like a lot of nutmeg mellows surprisingly when frozen. This unusual ice cream proves that freshly-grated nutmeg is destined for greater things than the finishing touch on eggnog. When paired with tart lemons and fragrant vanilla, the result is ethereal.

1 Using the pointed tip of a sharp knife, split the vanilla pod in half lengthways and scrape the tiny black seeds into a heavy medium saucepan. Add the cream and bring to the simmer over a medium heat. Remove from the heat, cover, and let stand at room temperature for 30 minutes to blend the flavours.

2 In a large bowl, whisk together the sugar and egg yolks until well-blended. Gradually whisk in about 240ml (8fl oz) of the warm cream. Return the egg mixture to the saucepan, reduce the heat to medium-low, and cook, stirring, until the custard thickens enough to coat the back of a spoon, 75–80°C. Do not let boil, or the egg yolks will curdle.

3 Sieve the custard into a bowl, pressing through as many of the vanilla seeds as you can. Cover and refrigerate for at least 3 hours, or until the custard is very cold. Stir in the lemon rind, lemon juice, and grated nutmeg.

4 Pour the custard into the canister of an ice cream maker and freeze according to the manufacturer's directions. Transfer to a covered container and freeze until it is firm enough to scoop, at least 3 hours or overnight.

INGREDIENTS

1 vanilla pod, split in half

900ml (1¾ pints) single cream

450g (14oz) sugar

6 egg yolks

1tbsp grated lemon rind

120ml (4fl oz) fresh lemon juice (3 or 4 lemons)

1tbsp freshly-grated nutmeg

Makes about 1¼ litres (2½ pints)

COOL TIPS FOR SUCCESS

To avoid curdling in ice creams that are custard-based, the egg yolks are first "tempered": some of the hot milk or cream is slowly whisked into the yolks to warm them gently before whisking them into the rest of the hot liquid.

Cinnamon-Basil Ice Cream

Chef Jerry Traunfeld of The Herbfarm restaurant outside of Seattle, Washington created this enchanting flavour of ice cream. If you have a garden and grow cinnamon basil, by all means use it here. Serve with a light dusting of cinnamon.

1 Bring the milk to the simmer in a heavy medium saucepan over a medium heat. Add the basil and cinnamon stick, cover, and remove from the heat. Let steep for 15 minutes, then strain through a sieve, pressing down on the basil to extract all the liquid.

2 Whisk together the egg yolks and sugar in a large mixing bowl. Slowly whisk in the cinnamon-basil flavoured milk. Return to the saucepan and cook over a medium heat, stirring constantly with a silicone spatula or wooden spoon, until the custard thickens enough to coat the back of a spoon, 75–80°C. Do not let boil, or the egg yolks will curdle.

3 Immediately pour the custard back into the mixing bowl and let cool, either over a larger bowl of ice with a little water or in the refrigerator, until the custard is very cold. Whisk in the double cream.

4 Pour the custard into the canister of an ice cream maker and freeze according to the manufacturer's directions. Transfer the ice cream to a covered container and freeze until it is firm enough to scoop, at least 3 hours or overnight.

INGREDIENTS

600ml (1¼ pints) milk
1 bunch (about 30g or 1oz) of fresh basil, well-rinsed
1 cinnamon stick
8 egg yolks
225g (8oz) sugar
360ml (12fl oz) double cream

Makes about 1½ litres (3 pints)

Almost-Instant Banana Ice Cream

Sweetened condensed milk, single cream, and double cream combine to make a lush ice cream that needs no cooked custard. Since only the condensed milk needs chilling here, your base should be ready in an hour or less. For best flavour, be sure the bananas are very ripe, nicely speckled with brown spots.

1 In a large bowl, whisk together the single cream, sweetened condensed milk, double cream, and vanilla extract until well-blended. Cover and refrigerate for 1 hour, or until cold.

2 Pour into the canister of an ice cream maker and freeze according to the manufacturer's directions until the ice cream is softly frozen.

3 Mash the bananas with the lemon juice. Add to the ice cream maker and continue to process for 2 minutes longer. Transfer the ice cream to a covered container and freeze until it is firm enough to scoop, at least 3 hours or overnight.

INGREDIENTS

500ml (16fl oz) single cream
1 can (397g or 14oz) sweetened condensed milk
240ml (8fl oz) double cream
1tsp vanilla extract
2 very ripe bananas
2tsp fresh lemon or lime juice

Makes about 1 litre (2 pints)

VARIATION

Almost-Instant Strawberry Ice Cream: Substitute 225g (8oz) fresh, crushed strawberries for the bananas.

Butter Pecan Ice Cream

There really is butter in this sumptuous ice cream, which gives it extra richness and body. If you can find fresh southern pecans, their sweetness and flavour will really stand out here.

INGREDIENTS

115g (4oz) pecan halves and pieces

500ml (16fl oz) milk

240ml (8fl oz) double cream

140g (5oz) granulated sugar

75g (2½oz) dark brown sugar

85g (3oz) unsalted butter, cut into pieces

4 egg yolks

1tsp vanilla extract

¼tsp salt

Makes about 1 litre (2 pints)

1 Preheat the oven to 160°C (325°F/Gas 3). Spread out the pecans in a baking pan and bake for 7–10 minutes, or until lightly toasted and fragrant. Set aside to cool.

2 In a heavy medium saucepan, combine the milk, cream, granulated sugar, and brown sugar. Cook over a medium heat, stirring occasionally for about 5 minutes, until the sugars dissolve and the mixture is hot.

3 In a heavy small saucepan, cook the butter over a medium heat, stirring occasionally, until very lightly browned. Remove from the heat, but keep warm.

4 Whisk the egg yolks with the salt lightly in a medium bowl. Gradually whisk the browned butter and then about 240ml (8fl oz) of the warm cream into the yolks. Return the egg mixture to the saucepan, reduce the heat to medium-low, and cook, stirring, until the custard thickens enough to coat the back of a spoon, 75–80°C. Do not let boil, or the egg yolks will curdle.

5 Sieve the custard into a bowl. Cover and refrigerate until the custard is very cold, at least 6 hours or as long as 2 days. Whisk in the vanilla extract.

6 Pour into the canister of an ice cream maker and freeze according to the manufacturer's directions. Add the pecans and process for 1 minute longer. Transfer the ice cream to a covered container and freeze until it is firm enough to scoop, 3 hours or overnight.

Eggnog Ice Cream with Hot Buttered Rum Sauce

Dust off that old punch bowl and serve scoops of this spiked ice cream in little cups, drizzled with Hot Buttered Rum Sauce and garnished with a dollop of whipped cream and a grating of fresh nutmeg. Because the flavour is as rich as you expect eggnog to be, servings should be small.

1 In a heavy medium saucepan, combine the milk, cream, and sugar. Cook over a medium heat, stirring occasionally, until the sugar dissolves and the mixture is hot, about 5 minutes.

2 Whisk the egg yolks lightly in a medium bowl. Gradually whisk in about 240ml (8fl oz) of the hot cream. Return the egg mixture to the saucepan. Reduce the heat to medium-low, and cook, stirring, until the custard thickens enough to coat the back of a spoon, 75–80°C. Do not let boil, or the egg yolks will curdle.

3 Sieve the custard into a bowl and stir in the rum. Cover and refrigerate until the custard is very cold, at least 6 hours or as long as 2 days. Stir in the vanilla extract and grated nutmeg.

4 Pour the custard into the canister of an ice cream maker and freeze according to the manufacturer's directions. Transfer the ice cream to a covered container and freeze until it is firm enough to scoop, at least 3 hours or overnight. To serve, drizzle Hot Buttered Rum Sauce over each serving and dust with a pinch of grated nutmeg.

Hot Buttered Rum Sauce

In a small saucepan, melt the butter over a medium heat. Whisk in the brown sugar, cream, golden syrup, and salt. Bring to the boil and cook for 1 minute. Remove from the heat and stir in the rum. Use at once, or cover and refrigerate for up to 2 days.

INGREDIENTS

500ml (16fl oz) milk
360ml (12fl oz) double cream
140g (5oz) sugar
4 egg yolks
3tbsp dark rum, such as Myers's
1tsp vanilla extract
¼tsp freshly grated nutmeg

Makes about 1 litre (2 pints)

Hot Buttered Rum Sauce

115g (4oz) unsalted butter, cut into pieces
225g (8oz) light brown sugar
120ml (4fl oz) double cream
2tbsp golden syrup
Pinch of salt
2tbsp dark rum, such as Myers's

Makes about 360ml (12fl oz)

Rum-Raisin Pumpkin Ice Cream

Unsweetened canned pumpkin for pies is the only kind to use for this special recipe. It's made from a variety of squash that yields exactly the right taste for this sweetly spiced dessert. Fresh pumpkin will not be intense enough. Serve the ice cream on its own or over a slice of Madeira cake or gingerbread.

1 In a nonreactive small saucepan, combine the raisins and rum. Bring to the simmer over a low heat. (Watch carefully, adjusting the heat as needed; if the alcohol gets too hot, it can ignite.) Remove from the heat and let cool. Set aside.

2 In a large bowl, gradually whisk the sugar into the cream until it dissolves. Whisk in the pumpkin, ginger, cinnamon, and cloves. Cover and refrigerate until cold, at least 2 hours or as long as 2 days.

3 Whisk the ice cream base to blend. Pour into the canister of an ice cream maker and freeze according to the manufacturer's directions. Add the raisins along with any remaining rum and process for 1 minute longer. Transfer the ice cream to a covered container and freeze until it is firm enough to scoop, at least 3 hours or overnight.

INGREDIENTS

175g (6oz) seedless raisins
120ml (4fl oz) dark rum, such as Myers's
450g (14oz) sugar
500ml (16fl oz) double cream
1 can (425g or 15oz) solid pack unsweetened pumpkin
¼tsp ground ginger
¼tsp ground cinnamon
¼tsp ground cloves

Makes about 1 litre (2 pints)

No-Cook Vanilla Ice Cream

In a hurry? Here's the recipe to turn to. Since there is no cooking, no eggs, and all the ingredients are cold to begin with, you can make home-made ice cream in less than half an hour, if your machine is up to it. The texture is a bit icier than custard-based ice creams, so the dessert is best served the same day it is made, but there is a lot to be said for instant gratification.

1 In a large bowl, combine the milk, cream, and salt. Gradually whisk in the sugar and vanilla extract. If you have time, cover and refrigerate for 1–2 hours to allow the flavours to develop.

2 Pour into the canister of an ice cream maker and freeze according to the manufacturer's directions. Transfer the ice cream to a covered container and freeze until it is firm enough to scoop, at least 3 hours or overnight.

INGREDIENTS

360ml (12fl oz) milk

360ml (12fl oz) double cream

Pinch of salt

140g (5oz) sugar

2tsp vanilla extract

Makes about 1 litre (2 pints)

VARIATION

No-Cook Chocolate Cookie Swirl Ice Cream: Prepare the No-Cook Vanilla Ice Cream above. After the ice cream is frozen according to the manufacturer's directions, with the machine on, add about 9 coarsely crushed creme-filled chocolate sandwich cookies, such as Oreos®, or chocolate cookies and process for 30–60 seconds, until just swirled through. Transfer to a covered container and freeze for at least 3 hours before serving.

White Chocolate Ice Cream with Bittersweet Fudge Ripple

When shopping for white chocolate, be sure to choose pure white chocolate. Cocoa butter should be listed as the primary ingredient on the label. To make plain white chocolate ice cream, simply omit the fudge swirl.

1 In a heavy nonreactive medium saucepan, combine the milk, cream, sugar, and salt. Bring to the simmer over a medium heat, stirring, until the sugar dissolves and the mixture is hot, about 5 minutes. Remove from the heat. Add the chopped white chocolate and whisk until melted and smooth.

2 Whisk the egg yolks lightly in a medium bowl. Gradually whisk in about 240ml (8fl oz) of the warm white chocolate cream. Gradually whisk the egg yolk–white chocolate mixture into the remaining cream in the pan. Reduce the heat to medium-low and cook, stirring, until the custard thickens enough to coat the back of a spoon, 75–80°C. Do not let boil, or the egg yolks will curdle.

3 Sieve the custard into a bowl. Let cool slightly, then cover and refrigerate until the custard is very cold, at least 6 hours or as long as 2 days. Stir in the vanilla extract.

4 Pour the custard into the canister of an ice cream maker and freeze according to the manufacturer's directions. With the machine on, pour in the Bittersweet Fudge Sauce and process for 30–60 seconds, or until marbled. Transfer the ice cream to a covered container and freeze until it is firm enough to scoop, at least 3 hours or overnight.

INGREDIENTS

360ml (12fl oz) milk

240ml (8fl oz) double cream

115g (4oz) sugar

Pinch of salt

115g (4oz) white chocolate, finely chopped

4 egg yolks

½tsp vanilla extract

240ml (8fl oz) Bittersweet Fudge Sauce (page 184)

Makes about 1 litre (2 pints)

Coconut Ice Cream
with Crystallised Ginger

Cool and refreshing, with a pleasant touch of heat from ginger, this ice cream is the perfect ending to any Asian-inspired or spicy meal. Serve plain or showered with toasted coconut.

1 Pour the coconut milk into a heavy medium saucepan, making sure to scrape in the thick part at the bottom; whisk to homogenise. Whisk in the cream, sugar, and salt. Cook over a medium heat, stirring occasionally, for 5 minutes, or until the sugar dissolves and the coconut cream is hot.

2 Whisk the egg yolks lightly in a medium bowl. Gradually whisk in about 240ml (8fl oz) of the warm coconut cream. Return the egg yolk mixture to the saucepan, reduce the heat to medium-low, and cook, stirring, until the custard thickens enough to coat the back of a spoon, 75–80°C. Do not let boil, or the egg yolks will curdle.

3 Sieve the coconut custard into a bowl and let cool to room temperature. Cover and refrigerate until very cold, at least 6 hours or as long as 2 days. Stir the ginger and vanilla extract into the coconut custard.

4 Pour the custard into the canister of an ice cream maker and freeze according to the manufacturer's directions. Transfer the ice cream to a covered container and freeze until it is firm enough to scoop, at least 3 hours or overnight.

INGREDIENTS

1 can (400ml or 13oz) unsweetened coconut milk
240ml (8fl oz) double cream
115g (4oz) sugar
¼tsp salt
3 egg yolks
3tbsp coarsely chopped crystallised ginger
1tsp vanilla extract

Makes about 1 litre (2 pints)

COOL TIPS FOR SUCCESS

Straining the cooked custard through a sieve ensures that no chewy bits of cooked egg will ruin the texture of your ice cream.

Green Tea Ice Cream

Green tea powder, which is called *matcha*, can be found in the international food section of some supermarkets, in Japanese markets, and online. It has a slightly smoky herbal taste with just a hint of bitterness and is a great antioxidant. As an ice cream, it's a good choice after a Chinese or Japanese meal, or when you want a subtle dessert that takes a back seat to the other courses.

1　In a large bowl, combine the milk and sugar. Whisk to dissolve the sugar. Whisk in the cream and salt.

2　Gradually whisk in the green tea powder 1tbsp at a time, blending until smooth. Stir in the vanilla extract. Cover and refrigerate for 1–2 hours to allow the flavours to develop.

3　Pour into the canister of an ice cream maker and freeze according to the manufacturer's directions. Transfer the ice cream to a covered container and freeze until it is firm enough to scoop, at least 3 hours or overnight.

INGREDIENTS

240ml (8fl oz) milk

175g (6oz) sugar

500ml (16fl oz) double cream

Pinch of salt

3tbsp green tea powder (matcha)

⅛tsp vanilla extract

Makes about 1 litre (2 pints)

Chocolate Custard Ice Cream

Rich, dark, silky, and smooth—this is everything chocolate ice cream should be. Because it calls for cocoa powder and plain dark chocolate, it's not too sweet.

1 In a heavy medium saucepan, combine the milk, cream, sugar, and salt. Bring to the simmer over a medium heat, stirring, for about 5 minutes, or until the sugar dissolves and the mixture is hot. Remove from the heat and whisk in the cocoa powder until well-blended. Whisk in the chopped chocolate until melted and smooth.

2 Whisk the egg yolks lightly in a medium bowl. Gradually whisk in about 240ml (8fl oz) of the warm chocolate cream. Whisk the egg mixture into the remaining chocolate cream in the pan, reduce the heat to medium-low, and cook, stirring, until the custard thickens enough to coat the back of a spoon, 75–80°C. Do not let boil, or the egg yolks will curdle. Sieve the chocolate custard into a bowl. Cover and refrigerate until the custard is very cold, at least 6 hours or as long as 2 days. Stir in the vanilla extract.

3 Pour the custard into the canister of an ice cream maker and freeze according to the manufacturer's directions. Transfer the ice cream to a covered container and freeze until firm enough to scoop, at least 3 hours or overnight.

INGREDIENTS

600ml (1¼ pints) milk
240ml (8fl oz) double cream
175g (6oz) sugar
Pinch of salt
4tbsp unsweetened cocoa powder
115g (4oz) plain dark chocolate, finely chopped
4 egg yolks
1½tsp vanilla extract

Makes about 1 litre (2 pints)

> ### VARIATION
>
> **Chocolate Custard Ice Cream with Marshmallow Swirl (pictured at right):** Follow the recipe as directed above, freezing the ice cream according to the manufacturer's directions. With the machine running, add half a 213g (7oz) jar of marshmallow fluff, one heaping spoonful at a time, processing for 30–60 seconds, or until just swirled through. Transfer the ice cream to a covered container and freeze until firm enough to scoop, at least 3 hours.

Coffee Ice Cream

This recipe comes from Christine Law, and was perfected during her nine years as executive pastry chef for Wolfgang Puck's Spago and Postrio restaurants in California. Excellent scooped up on its own, no one will object to a drizzle of chocolate sauce and an extra splash of Kahlúa.

1 Place the coffee beans in a plastic bag and crush with a rolling pin; do not grind the beans in a coffee mill. Combine the crushed coffee beans, cream, milk, and evaporated milk in a heavy medium saucepan. Warm over a medium-low heat until barely simmering. Remove from the heat, cover, and let steep for 30 minutes. Strain through a sieve lined with layers of muslin.

2 Pour the coffee cream into a clean saucepan and stir in half of the sugar. Return to a medium-low heat and cook, stirring to dissolve the sugar, until barely simmering.

3 In a large bowl with an electric mixer, whisk the egg yolks with the golden syrup and remaining sugar until fluffy. Slowly pour in 240ml (8fl oz) of the hot coffee cream in a thin stream. Whisk the egg yolk mixture into the remaining coffee cream in the saucepan. Cook over a medium heat, whisking vigorously, until the temperature reaches 75–80°C. Do not boil, or the egg yolks will curdle.

4 Immediately strain through a fine sieve into a heatproof bowl.

5 Set the bowl over a larger bowl filled with ice and a little water and whisk occasionally until cooled to lukewarm. Blend in the Kahlúa. Cover and refrigerate for at least 4 hours or overnight.

6 Pour the coffee custard into the canister of an ice cream maker and freeze according to the manufacturer's directions. Transfer to a covered container and freeze at least 3 hours or overnight.

INGREDIENTS

4tbsp dark roast whole coffee beans

360ml (12fl oz) double cream

240ml (8fl oz) milk

4tbsp light evaporated milk

140g (5oz) sugar

4 egg yolks

1tbsp golden syrup

2tsp Kahlúa (or other coffee liqueur) or 1tsp coffee extract

Makes about 750 ml (1½ pints)

Mint Chocolate Chunk Ice Cream

An infusion of fresh mint imparts a subtle yet distinctive flavour to this delectable ice cream. It's much more sophisticated than commercial brands pumped up with artificial flavour. Because we're so used to green mint ice cream, you can add a few drops of green food colouring, but it's optional.

1 In a heavy nonreactive medium saucepan, combine the single cream, double cream, mint, and lemon rind. Bring to the simmer over a medium heat. Remove from the heat, cover, and let stand at room temperature for 30 minutes to allow the flavours to steep. Add the sugar and salt. Return to medium heat and cook, stirring occasionally, until the sugar dissolves and the liquid is hot, about 5 minutes.

2 Whisk the egg yolks lightly in a medium bowl. Gradually whisk in about 240ml (8fl oz) of the warm mint cream. Whisk the egg yolk mixture into the mint cream remaining in the pan, reduce the heat to medium-low, and cook, stirring, until the custard thickens enough to coat the back of a spoon, 75–80°C. Do not let boil, or the egg yolks will curdle.

3 Sieve the custard into a bowl, pressing on the mint with the back of a spoon to release the flavour; then discard the mint and lemon rind. Stir in the food colouring if you are using it. Cover and refrigerate until the custard is very cold, at least 6 hours.

4 Pour the custard into the canister of an ice cream maker and freeze according to the manufacturer's directions. Add the chocolate chunks and process for about 1 minute, until incorporated. Transfer the ice cream to a covered container and freeze until firm enough to scoop, at least 3 hours or overnight.

INGREDIENTS

750ml (1½ pints) single cream

240ml (8fl oz) double cream

1 good handful of fresh mint sprigs, preferably peppermint, coarsely chopped stems and all

1 thin strip of lemon rind, about 5cm (2in) long and 1cm (½in) wide

175g (6oz) sugar

Pinch of salt

4 egg yolks

1–2 drops of green food colouring (optional)

115g (4oz) plain dark or mint-flavoured chocolate chunks

Makes about 1 litre (2 pints)

COOL TIPS FOR SUCCESS

When you chop chocolate even coarsely, tiny powder bits flake off. To avoid small specks of chocolate in the finished ice cream, place the chopped chocolate in a sieve and shake to remove any fine bits. Save the chocolate powder for the next time you are melting chocolate or making hot chocolate.

Gianduja Chocolate Chunk Gelato

Gianduja combines chocolate with hazelnuts. You can buy bottles of hazelnut syrup by mail order and online. For an extra fillip, sprinkle chopped gianduja or dark chocolate and toasted hazelnuts over each serving.

INGREDIENTS

115g (4oz) hazelnuts
600ml (1¼ pints) milk
5tbsp double cream
4 egg yolks
140g (5oz) sugar
Pinch of salt
60g (2oz) very bitter dark chocolate, finely chopped
1tbsp hazelnut liqueur, such as Frangelico®, or hazelnut syrup
½tsp vanilla extract
1 chocolate-hazelnut bar (100–115g or 3–4oz), or other gianduja, chopped into small chunks and then refrigerated until cold

Makes about 1 litre (2 pints)

1 Preheat the oven to 160°C (325°F/Gas 3). Toast the hazelnuts on a baking sheet for 10–12 minutes, until the nuts are lightly browned and fragrant. Rub the warm nuts in a tea towel to remove as much of the skin as possible. When cool, coarsely chop the nuts.

2 In a heavy medium saucepan, combine the milk and cream. Bring to the simmer over a medium heat. Stir in the chopped hazelnuts and remove from the heat. Cover and let stand at room temperature for 30 minutes to cool and allow the flavours to develop. Sieve to remove the nuts and return the hazelnut milk to the saucepan.

3 In a large bowl, whisk together the egg yolks, sugar, and salt until well-blended. Whisk about 240ml (8fl oz) of the warm hazelnut milk into the egg yolks. Whisk the egg yolk mixture into the remaining hazelnut milk in the saucepan. Cook over a medium-low heat, stirring, until the custard thickens enough to coat the back of a spoon, 75–80°C. Do not let boil, or the egg yolks will curdle.

4 Sieve the custard into a clean bowl. Add the dark chocolate and whisk until melted and smooth. Stir in the hazelnut liqueur. Cover and refrigerate until the custard is very cold, at least 6 hours or as long as 2 days. Stir in the vanilla extract.

5 Pour the custard into the canister of an ice cream maker and freeze according to the manufacturer's directions. Add the cold chocolate chunks and process for 1 minute longer. Transfer the gelato to a covered container and freeze until it is firm enough to scoop, 3 hours or overnight.

Chocolate-Chilli
Ice Cream

Creative cooks know that sweet and hot complement each other, and the Aztecs in Mexico long ago discovered how well fiery chillis and chocolate went together. Add a third element—cold—and you've got an irresistible as well as interesting flavour.

1 In a heavy medium saucepan, combine the cream, milk, sugar, and salt. Bring to the simmer over a medium heat, stirring, for about 5 minutes, or until the sugar dissolves and the mixture is hot.

2 Remove from the heat and whisk in the chilli powder and cinnamon. Add the chopped chocolate and whisk until melted and smooth. Cover and refrigerate for 3 hours, or until cold. Stir in the vanilla extract.

3 Pour into the canister of an ice cream maker and freeze according to the manufacturer's directions. Transfer the ice cream to a covered container and freeze until it is firm enough to scoop, at least 3 hours or overnight.

INGREDIENTS

500ml (16fl oz) double cream
240ml (8fl oz) milk
140g (5oz) sugar
Pinch of salt
1tsp chilli powder
½tsp ground cinnamon
225g (8oz) plain dark chocolate, finely chopped
1tsp vanilla extract

Makes about 1 litre (2 pints)

Espresso Bean Gelato with Toffee Bits

Espresso beans are simply coffee beans that have been darkly roasted. As with other coffee, the quality greatly affects the final flavour, so choose beans that are glossy and fragrant for this rich, silky ice cream.

1 Place the espresso beans in a heavy-duty ziplock plastic bag. Coarsely crush with a rolling pin or under a heavy pan. Do not grind in a coffee mill.

2 In a heavy medium saucepan, combine the crushed espresso beans with the milk and cream. Bring to the simmer over a medium heat. Remove from the heat, cover, and let steep at room temperature for 30 minutes.

3 Stir in the sugar and salt. Return to medium heat and cook, stirring occasionally, until the sugar dissolves and the mixture is hot, about 5 minutes.

4 Whisk the egg yolks lightly in a medium bowl. Gradually whisk in 240ml (8fl oz) of the warm espresso cream. Whisk the egg yolk mixture into the remaining espresso cream in the saucepan, reduce the heat to medium-low, and cook, stirring, until the custard thickens enough to coat the back of a spoon, 75–80°C. Do not let boil, or the egg yolks will curdle. Sieve the custard into a bowl. Cover and refrigerate for 4 hours, or until very cold. Stir in the vanilla extract.

5 Pour the custard into the canister of an ice cream maker and freeze according to the manufacturer's directions. Add the chilled toffee and process for 1 minute longer, or until incorporated. Transfer the gelato to a covered container and freeze until it is firm enough to scoop, at least 3 hours or overnight.

INGREDIENTS

60g (2oz) espresso coffee beans

600ml (1¼ pints) milk

120ml (4fl oz) double cream

175g (6oz) sugar

Pinch of salt

6 egg yolks

1½tsp vanilla extract

60g (2oz) crushed chocolate-covered toffee, chilled, or crumbled biscotti

Makes about 1 litre (2 pints)

"it's amazing how quickly you recover from misery when someone offers you ice cream."

–Neil Simon, *Brighton Beach Memoirs*

light ice creams,
ice milks,
& sherbets

Quick Toffee-Pecan Light Ice Cream

With a bottle of toffee sauce in your pantry and a package of chopped pecans, you've got all the makings you need for a delectable ice cream that requires no custard. The sticky toffee adds all the body that's needed for a rich and creamy dessert.

1 Preheat the oven to 160°C (325°F/Gas 3). Spread out the pecans in a baking pan and bake for 7–10 minutes, or until lightly toasted and fragrant. Transfer to a plate and set aside to cool.

2 In a large bowl, combine the single cream, toffee sauce, vanilla extract, and salt. Whisk to blend. Cover and refrigerate for 2 hours, or until very cold.

3 Pour into the canister of an ice cream maker and freeze according to the manufacturer's directions. Add the pecans and process for 1 minute longer, or until incorporated. Transfer the ice cream to a covered container and freeze until it is firm enough to scoop, at least 3 hours or overnight.

INGREDIENTS

85g (3oz) coarsely chopped pecans

900ml (1¾ pints) single cream

1 bottle (320g or 10oz) toffee sauce

2tsp vanilla extract

Pinch of salt

Makes about 1½ litres (3 pints)

Maple Walnut
Light Ice Cream

Most maple walnut ice creams are custard-based and exceptionally rich. But take the same excellent ingredients—Grade A amber maple syrup, fresh nuts, and pure vanilla extract—combine them with single cream instead of double cream, omit the egg yolks, and you've got a delightful dessert with half the fat.

1 Preheat the oven to 180°C (350°F/Gas 4). Spread out the walnuts on a baking sheet. Toast in the oven, stirring once or twice, for 8–10 minutes or until lightly browned and fragrant. Set aside to cool.

2 In a large bowl, combine the single cream, maple syrup, vanilla extract, and salt. If you have time, refrigerate for 1–2 hours to allow the flavours to develop.

3 Pour into the canister of an ice cream maker and freeze according to the manufacturer's directions. Add the walnuts and process for 1 minute longer, or until incorporated. Transfer the ice cream to a covered container and freeze until it is firm enough to scoop, at least 3 hours or overnight.

INGREDIENTS

115g (4oz) coarsely chopped walnuts

750ml (1½ pints) single cream

240ml (8fl oz) pure maple syrup

1tsp vanilla extract

Pinch of salt

Makes about 1 litre (2 pints)

COOL TIPS FOR SUCCESS

Fill your ice cream machine no more than the manufacturer recommends. Some air will be incorporated during the freezing process, and the ice cream needs room to expand. This aeration process, called overrun, improves the texture of the ice cream.

Lavender Ice Milk

It's only recently that cooks have realized lavender's potential for adding an evocative floral note to many preparations. In a funny way, it's a flavour that's both trendy and timelessly classical. To release lavender's essential oils, crush the dried buds with a pestle and mortar or grind them in an electric spice mill.

1 Put the milk in a heavy medium saucepan with the sugar and lavender. Warm over a medium heat, stirring to dissolve the sugar, until small bubbles begin to appear around the edges of the pan. Remove from the heat, cover, and let steep at room temperature for 30 minutes.

2 Pour the lavender milk into a covered container and refrigerate until cold, 1–2 hours. Whisk in the lemon juice.

3 Pour into the canister of an ice cream maker and freeze according to the manufacturer's directions. Transfer the ice milk to a covered container and freeze until it is firm enough to scoop, at least 3 hours or overnight.

INGREDIENTS

900ml (1¾ pints) full fat or semi-skimmed milk

350g (12oz) sugar

1tbsp dried lavender, finely crushed

1tbsp fresh lemon juice

Makes about 1¼ litres (2½ pints)

COOL TIPS FOR SUCCESS

For best results purchase the culinary "Provence" lavender buds that are available at many gourmet shops and mail-order sources. It has a very low camphor level, a delicate floral note, and a subtle flavour. Other varieties can taste medicinal.

Honey Light Ice Cream with Roasted Almonds

When using only three ingredients, it's especially important those items be of the highest quality. The honey in this recipe provides sweetness as well as body, so check your local farmers' market or apiary for a deep variety that's full of flavour.

1 In a large bowl, whisk together the single cream and honey until well-blended. Cover and refrigerate until cold, about 1 hour.

2 Pour into the canister of an ice cream maker and freeze according to the manufacturer's directions. Add the almonds and process for 1 minute longer. Transfer the ice cream to a covered container and freeze until it is firm enough to scoop, at least 4 hours or overnight.

INGREDIENTS

900ml (1¾ pints) single cream

240ml (8fl oz) honey, preferably wildflower, linden, or chestnut honey

85g (3oz) honey-roasted or plain almonds, coarsely chopped

Makes about 1¼ litres (2½ pints)

COOL TIPS FOR SUCCESS

Most ice cream makers are designed with a feed tube on the lid specifically for adding ingredients at the end. When the ice cream is done, pour your "add-ins" through the feed tube and process until incorporated, usually 30–60 seconds. To ensure chocolate or toffee keeps its integrity, freeze the bits briefly before adding.

Drambuie Ice Milk

Drambuie is a Scotch whiskey-based liqueur sweetened with honey and flavoured with herbs. The crème fraîche adds richness, as well as a pleasant tartness, so this is best served in single-scoop portions, with a small glass of Drambuie on the side or over the top.

1 In a heavy small saucepan, bring the Drambuie to the simmer over a medium to medium-low heat. Cook until the liquid is reduced to about 4tbsp. (Watch carefully, adjusting the heat as needed; if the alcohol gets too hot, it can ignite.) Remove from the heat and transfer to a medium bowl. Stir in the sugar until dissolved. Let cool to room temperature.

2 Whisk in the milk. Cover and refrigerate until cold, at least 3 hours.

3 Whisk in the crème fraîche until well-blended. Pour into the canister of an ice cream maker and freeze according to the manufacturer's directions. Transfer the ice milk to a covered container and freeze until it is firm enough to scoop, at least 3 hours or overnight.

INGREDIENTS

120ml (4fl oz) Drambuie liqueur

175g (6oz) sugar

240ml (8fl oz) cold milk

1 container (200ml or 7½fl oz) crème fraîche

Makes about 750ml (1½ pints)

Strawberry Dream
Light Ice Cream

Choose the ripest fresh berries you can for this luscious no-cook ice cream, but trim off any bruised or damaged bits. If you use frozen, be sure to include any juices.

1 Working in batches if needed, purée the berries with half the sugar in a food processor or blender until smooth.

2 In a large bowl, whisk together the strawberry purée, single cream, orange extract, and remaining sugar. If you have time, cover and refrigerate for 1–2 hours to allow the flavours to develop.

3 Whisk the strawberry base to blend. Pour into the canister of an ice cream maker and freeze according to the manufacturer's directions. Transfer the ice cream to a covered container and freeze until it is firm enough to scoop, at least 4 hours or overnight.

INGREDIENTS

675g (1½lb) very ripe fresh strawberries, stemmed, or 2 packages (1lb each) frozen unsweetened strawberries, partially thawed

350g (12oz) sugar

500ml (16fl oz) single cream

1tsp orange extract

Makes about 1 litre (2 pints)

Clementine-Buttermilk Sherbet with Raspberry Swirl

Citrus is a delicious complement to tangy buttermilk. Health food stores and many supermarkets now carry excellent fresh fruit juices in their refrigerated section. Faced with the prospect of juicing about 16 clementines to get 2 cups of juice, you may opt for convenience. If plain clementine juice is not available, try a blend like orange-clementine.

1 In a food processor or blender, purée the raspberries with any juices until smooth. Strain through a medium sieve into a small nonreactive saucepan to remove the seeds. Press through as much of the fruit and juice as you can. Stir in 4tbsp of the sugar. Cook over a medium-low heat, stirring often, until the raspberry purée thickens, about 10 minutes. Remove from the heat and let cool to room temperature; then cover and refrigerate until cold, at least 1 hour.

2 In a large bowl, combine the remaining 280g (10oz) sugar with the buttermilk and clementine juice. Stir until the sugar dissolves.

3 Pour the clementine-buttermilk base into the canister of an ice cream maker and freeze according to the manufacturer's directions. Add the raspberry purée and process for 30–45 seconds, or just until swirled through. Transfer the sherbet to a covered container and freeze until it is firm enough to scoop, at least 4 hours or overnight.

INGREDIENTS

1 packet (300g or 10oz) frozen unsweetened raspberries, thawed

350g (12oz) sugar

500ml (16fl oz) cold low-fat buttermilk, or 500ml (16fl oz) milk, mixed with 1tbsp lemon juice or vinegar

500ml (16 fl oz) cold clementine juice

Makes about 1¼ litres (2½ pints)

COOL TIPS FOR SUCCESS

When creating a swirl with a sauce, add after the ice cream is done and churn for 30–60 seconds, until only partially blended. For a more defined swirl, do not add the sauce to the ice cream machine. Instead, working quickly, layer the finished ice cream and the sauce in a freezer container and run a blunt knife through the mixture several times, folding slightly, to create a marbleised effect.

Orange Sherbet

Don't expect the brilliant orange of some commercial brands of orange sherbet here. While the flavour is distinctive, the colour is closest to cream. Any kind of orange juice can be used—fresh, frozen, reconstituted—but if it has pulp, strain before adding to achieve sherbet's characteristically smooth texture.

1 In a large bowl, combine the orange juice, sugar, and golden syrup. Stir to dissolve the sugar. Cover and refrigerate for 2 hours, or until very cold.

2 Whisk in the single cream or milk, and orange extract.

3 Pour into the canister of an ice cream maker and freeze according to the manufacturer's directions. Transfer the sherbet to a covered container and freeze until it is firm enough to scoop, at least 3 hours or overnight.

INGREDIENTS

600ml (1¼ pints) orange juice

75g (2½oz) sugar

1tbsp golden syrup

240ml (8fl oz) single cream or milk

¼tsp orange extract

Makes about 1 litre (2 pints)

Lime Sherbet

Of course, freshly squeezed fruit is best, but with bottled or frozen lime juice available year round in the supermarket, it's nice to know you don't have to spend half an hour squeezing dozens of limes. To make an instant frozen lime pie, pack the sherbet from the ice cream maker into a digestive cracker crust and return to the freezer. Just before serving, top the pie with sweetened whipped cream.

INGREDIENTS

240ml (8fl oz) lime juice
4tbsp sugar
120ml (4fl oz) golden syrup
1tbsp finely grated lime rind
1 can (397g or 14oz)
sweetened condensed milk

Makes about 700ml (1½ pints)

1   In a large bowl, combine the lime juice and sugar. Stir to dissolve the sugar, then blend in the golden syrup and lime rind. Cover and refrigerate for 1–2 hours, or until very cold. Whisk in the condensed milk.

2   Pour into the canister of an ice cream maker and freeze according to the manufacturer's directions. Transfer the sherbet to a covered container and freeze until it is firm enough to scoop, at least 3 hours or overnight.

Banana Split
Light Ice Cream

What could be better than all the flavours of a banana split locked up in a scoop of ice cream? This immensely satisfying flavour needs absolutely no garnish, though a single maraschino cherry on top would be a winsome touch.

1 Preheat the oven to 160°C (325°F/Gas 3). Spread out the pecans in a small baking dish and toast in the oven for 5–10 minutes, or until fragrant and very lightly browned. Transfer to a dish and let cool.

2 In a large bowl, combine the bananas, orange juice, sugar, and golden syrup. Mash with a fork to a coarse purée. Cover with cling film pressed directly onto the surface so the bananas do not discolour. Refrigerate for 1 hour, or until cold.

3 Mix in the single cream and vanilla extract. Pour into the canister of an ice cream maker and freeze according to the manufacturer's directions. Add the pecans, chocolate chips, and cherries and process for 1 minute longer, or until incorporated. Transfer the ice cream to a covered container and freeze until it is firm enough to scoop, at least 3 hours or overnight.

INGREDIENTS

45g (1½oz) coarsely chopped pecans

2 very ripe medium bananas

1tbsp orange juice

115g (4oz) sugar

2tbsp golden syrup

500ml (16fl oz) single cream

2tsp vanilla extract

60g (2oz) plain chocolate chips

6 maraschino cherries, stemmed and chopped

Makes about 750ml (1½ pints)

Boysenberry Buttermilk Sherbet

Boysenberries are an intense sweet dark berry, with a lot more flavour than blackberries. They are imported to the UK from New Zealand but if you can't find them, blackberries or raspberries can be substituted. As in baking, buttermilk, rather than ordinary milk or cream, adds a wonderful hint of tang with very little fat.

1 If using fresh berries, rinse gently and drain in a colander. Pick over to remove any badly bruised or mouldy fruit.

2 In a food processor or blender, combine the boysenberries, 175g (6oz) sugar, and the lemon juice. Purée until smooth.

3 Sieve the berry mixture into a large bowl to remove the seeds, pressing through as much of the juice and fruit as you can. Stir in the golden syrup. Taste and add more sugar, 1tbsp at a time, if you think it's needed. Cover and refrigerate for 2 hours, or until very cold. Whisk in the buttermilk.

4 Pour into the canister of an ice cream maker and freeze according to the manufacturer's directions. Transfer the sherbet to a covered container and freeze until it is firm enough to scoop, at least 3 hours or overnight.

INGREDIENTS

550g (1¼lb) fresh boysenberries or frozen unsweetened raspberries or blackberries, partially thawed

175–225g (6–8oz) sugar

1tsp fresh lemon juice

1tbsp golden syrup

500ml (16fl oz) cold buttermilk or 500ml (16fl oz) milk mixed with 1tbsp lemon juice or vinegar

Makes about 1 litre (2 pints)

Ginger Bite Light Ice Cream

Pungent ground dried ginger and mellower crystallised ginger add up to a grown-up ice cream with a bit of a bite. Dress up, if you like, with a drizzle of Bittersweet Fudge Sauce (page 184) and pass a plate of buttery Scottish shortbread or sugar cookies on the side.

1 In a large bowl, whisk together the single cream, sugar, ground ginger, and vanilla extract. If you have time, cover the mixture and refrigerate for an hour to allow the flavours to develop.

2 Pour the mixture into the canister of an ice cream maker and freeze according to the manufacturer's directions. Add the crystallised ginger and process for 1 minute longer. Transfer the ice cream to a covered container and freeze until it is firm enough to scoop, at least 3 hours or overnight.

INGREDIENTS

900ml (1¾ pints) single cream
350g (12oz) sugar
2tsp ground ginger
1tsp vanilla extract
115g (4oz) chopped crystallised ginger

Makes about 1¼ litres (2½ pints)

COOL TIPS FOR SUCCESS

Many sorbets and ice creams that are non-custard based become hard in the freezer. Let them stand at room temperature for 5 minutes until softened enough to scoop.

Peppermint
Light Ice Cream

Ordinary white round peppermints combine with peppermint extract for a bracing frozen dessert especially for mint lovers. For the full treatment, serve with Peppermint Fudge Sauce (page 117).

1 In a heavy medium saucepan, bring the milk to the simmer over a medium heat. Cook, stirring, for about 3 minutes, or until the mixture is hot and bubbles just begin to form at the edges. Remove from the heat.

2 Whisk the egg yolks lightly in a medium bowl. Gradually whisk in about 240ml (8fl oz) of the warm milk. Return the egg mixture to the saucepan, reduce the heat to medium-low, and cook, stirring, until the custard thickens enough to coat the back of a spoon, 75–80°C. Do not let boil, or the egg yolks will curdle.

3 Sieve the custard into a large bowl. Whisk in the sweetened condensed milk. Cover and refrigerate until the custard is very cold, at least 4 hours. Stir in half of the crushed peppermints, the vanilla extract, and the peppermint extract.

4 Pour the custard into the canister of an ice cream maker and freeze according to the manufacturer's directions. Add the remaining crushed peppermints and process for 1 minute longer, or until incorporated. Transfer the ice cream to a covered container and freeze until it is firm enough to scoop, at least 4 hours or overnight.

INGREDIENTS

600ml (1¼ pints) whole milk

2 egg yolks

1 can (397g or 14 oz) sweetened condensed milk

140g (5oz) crushed peppermints

1tsp vanilla extract

½tsp peppermint extract

Makes about 1 litre (2 pints)

Frozen Hot Chocolate

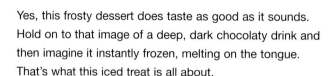

Yes, this frosty dessert does taste as good as it sounds. Hold on to that image of a deep, dark chocolaty drink and then imagine it instantly frozen, melting on the tongue. That's what this iced treat is all about.

1 In a heavy large saucepan, combine the single cream, sugar, and salt. Bring to the simmer over a medium heat, stirring, for about 5 minutes, or until the sugar dissolves and the mixture is hot. Remove from the heat and whisk in the cocoa powder until well-blended. Add the chopped chocolate and stir until melted and smooth. Let stand for 15 minutes to cool slightly, then whisk in the vanilla extract. Cover and refrigerate for 2 hours, or until very cold.

2 Stir the chocolate base to blend and pour into the canister of an ice cream maker. Freeze according to the manufacturer's directions. Eat at once while soft and somewhat slushy or transfer to a covered container and freeze for up to 4 hours.

3 Serve in large goblets or mugs, with a spoon and a straw. Top with marshmallows or whipped cream, and a dusting of shaved chocolate or a few chocolate curls.

INGREDIENTS

750ml (1½ pints) single cream

175g sugar

Pinch of salt

50g (1¾oz) unsweetened cocoa powder

60g (2oz) plain dark chocolate, finely chopped

1tsp vanilla extract

Marshmallows or whipped cream, for garnish

Shaved chocolate or Chocolate Curls (page 187), for garnish

Makes about 1 litre (2 pints)

Dark Chocolate Ice Milk

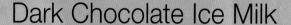

In between an ice cream and a sorbet, this light chocolate frozen dessert is both refreshing and satisfying. Adorn, if you like, with a drizzle of chocolate or raspberry sauce.

1 In a heavy medium saucepan, whisk the cocoa powder into the water until smooth. Whisk in the sugar, milk, and salt. Bring to the boil over a medium heat, stirring constantly, until the sugar is dissolved. Remove from the heat. Whisk in the golden syrup.

2 Cover and refrigerate for at least 4 hours, or until very cold. Whisk in the vanilla extract to blend.

3 Pour into the canister of an ice cream maker and freeze according to the manufacturer's directions. Transfer the ice milk to a covered container and freeze until it is firm enough to scoop, at least 3 hours or overnight.

INGREDIENTS

60g (2oz) unsweetened cocoa powder

360ml (12fl oz) water

225g (8oz) sugar

240ml (8fl oz) milk

Pinch of salt

1tbsp golden syrup

½tsp vanilla extract

Makes about 1 litre (2 pints)

Peanut Butter Light Ice Cream

Creamy peanut butter adds body, texture, and richness to this egg-free ice cream. It's luscious served *au natural*, and even better drizzled with your favourite chocolate sauce and showered with chopped roasted peanuts.

1 In a large bowl, combine the single cream, sugar, and salt. Whisk until well-blended. Gradually whisk in the peanut butter and vanilla extract. If you have time, cover and refrigerate for 1–2 hours to allow the flavours to develop.

2 Pour into the canister of an ice cream maker and freeze according to the manufacturer's directions. Transfer to a covered container and freeze for 1–4 hours before serving.

INGREDIENTS

750ml (1½ pints) single cream

140g (5oz) sugar

Pinch of salt

185g (6½oz) smooth peanut butter

1tsp vanilla extract

Makes about 1 litre (2 pints)

COOL TIPS FOR SUCCESS

Do not use an "old-fashioned" or "natural" peanut butter, which separates and becomes oily.

"enjoy your ice cream while
it's on your plate–
that's my philosophy."

–playwright Thornton Wilder

frozen yoghurts
& soya ice milks

Jamaican Banana Frozen Yoghurt

Bananas, lime, and coconut conjure up a great cold dessert for a warm summer night. To be sure the flavour is as intense as it should be, plan ahead so your bananas are overripe; the skins should be heavily speckled with brown spots.

1 Combine the sugar and water in a small saucepan. Cook over a medium heat, stirring until the sugar dissolves. Boil the syrup without stirring for 2 minutes. Pour into a large heatproof bowl and let cool.

2 Add the bananas and mash with a fork until no large chunks remain. Stir in the yoghurt, lime juice, and coconut extract. Cover and refrigerate for 2 hours, or until cold.

3 Pour the yoghurt base into the canister of an ice cream maker and freeze according to the manufacturer's directions. Transfer the frozen yoghurt to a covered container and freeze until it is firm enough to scoop, at least 4 hours or overnight.

INGREDIENTS

225g (8oz) sugar
240ml (8fl oz) water
2 overripe medium bananas
500g (1lb) plain yoghurt
1½tsp fresh lime juice
1tsp coconut extract

Makes about 1 litre (2 pints)

Golden Vanilla-Apricot Frozen Yoghurt

Lyle's Golden Syrup contributes a caramelised quality that simply can't be matched. If you prefer, substitute a good, flavourful honey for the golden syrup.

1 Place the chopped apricots in a bowl and add enough hot water to cover. Let stand for about 15 minutes to soften. Drain well. Cover and refrigerate until needed.

2 In a medium bowl, whisk together the yoghurt, syrup, and vanilla extract until well-blended. If you have time, cover and refrigerate the yoghurt base for 1–2 hours to allow the flavours to develop.

3 Pour the yoghurt base into the canister of an ice cream maker and freeze according to the manufacturer's directions. Add the chopped apricots and process for 1 minute longer, or until incorporated. Serve at once while still soft, or transfer to a covered container and freeze for 1–4 hours before serving.

INGREDIENTS

85g (3oz) finely chopped dried apricots

675g (1½lb) plain yoghurt

240ml (8fl oz) Lyle's Golden Syrup or honey

2tsp vanilla extract

Makes about 1 litre (2 pints)

Toasted Almond and Apricot Frozen Yoghurt

Apricots and almonds are a perfect pairing. Here they transform low-fat yoghurt into a stellar dessert that's lean and luscious at the same time.

1 Preheat the oven to 160°C (325°F/Gas 3). Spread out the almonds on a baking sheet and toast in the oven for 8–10 minutes, stirring once or twice, until lightly browned and fragrant. Transfer the nuts to a dish and let cool.

2 Drain the apricots, reserving 4tbsp of the syrup. Chop 3 apricot halves into bite-sized pieces; refrigerate until needed. In a food processor, purée the remaining apricots until smooth. Scrape into a large bowl.

3 Add the reserved apricot syrup, the yoghurt, brown sugar, lemon juice, almond extract, and salt to the puréed apricots. Mix until well-blended. Cover and refrigerate for 2 hours, or until very cold.

4 Pour the yoghurt base into the canister of an ice cream maker and freeze according to the manufacturer's directions. Add the reserved apricots and toasted almonds and process for 1 minute longer or until incorporated. Transfer the frozen yoghurt to a covered container and freeze until it is firm enough to scoop, at least 4 hours or overnight.

INGREDIENTS

60g (2oz) flaked almonds, coarsely chopped

2 cans (227g each, or 1 16oz can) apricot halves in syrup

450g (1lb) low-fat custard-style vanilla yoghurt

115g (4oz) light brown sugar

1tsp fresh lemon juice

½tsp almond extract

Pinch of salt

Makes about 1 litre (2 pints)

Lemon Curd Frozen Yoghurt

Here's a delightful lemon frozen dessert that can be thrown together in minutes. It's good on its own; sublime with a drizzle of Raspberry Sauce.

1 In a medium bowl, combine the yoghurt, sugar, and lemon rind. Stir to dissolve the sugar. If you have time, cover and refrigerate for 1–2 hours to allow the flavours to develop.

2 Pour the yoghurt into the canister of an ice cream maker and freeze according to the manufacturer's directions. Serve at once while still soft or transfer to a covered container and freeze for 1–4 hours before serving.

Raspberry Sauce

1 If using fresh berries, rinse gently and drain in a colander. Pick over to remove any bruised or mouldy fruit.

2 In a food processor or blender, purée the raspberries until smooth. Strain through a medium sieve into a bowl to remove the seeds. Press through as much of the fruit and juices as you can. Stir in the sugar and lemon juice. Let stand for 2–3 minutes, or until the sugar dissolves. Taste and stir in more sugar if needed. Serve at once or cover and refrigerate for up to 3 days. Freeze for longer storage. Serve chilled or at room temperature.

INGREDIENTS

675g (1½lb) lemon curd yoghurt
140–175g (5–6oz) sugar, to taste
Finely grated rind of 2 lemons

Makes about 750ml (1½ pints)

Raspberry Sauce

280g (10oz) fresh or thawed frozen unsweetened raspberries
3tbsp sugar
1tsp fresh lemon juice

Makes about 300ml (10fl oz)

VARIATION

Lemon-Ginger Frozen Yoghurt: When the yoghurt reaches the soft-serve stage, add about 115g (4oz) of finely chopped crystallised ginger and process for 1 minute longer or until incorporated.

Pink Grapefruit Soya Sherbet

Dairy free, this delightful sweet-tart sherbet gets its touch of creaminess from silken tofu. Best of all, no one will know it's there unless you tell them.

1 In a food processor or blender, combine the grapefruit juice, sugar, and tofu. Process until smooth. Scrape the mixture into a large bow!. Cover and refrigerate for 2 hours, or until very cold.

2 Stir to blend and pour into the canister of an ice cream maker. Freeze according to the manufacturer's directions. Eat at once or transfer to a covered container and freeze for 1–4 hours before serving.

INGREDIENTS

750ml (1½ pints) fresh ruby red or pink grapefruit juice

225g (8oz) sugar

350g (12oz) silken tofu

Makes about 1¼ litres (2½ pints)

COOL TIPS FOR SUCCESS

To prevent ice crystals from forming when ice cream is taken in and out of the freezer, cover any open container with cling film pressed directly onto the surface of the ice cream before closing the lid.

Spiced Plum Frozen Yoghurt

Santa Rosa plums, those firm black plums uniformly sweet and not too tart, are the first choice here, though other varieties could be substituted. Plums contain plenty of pectin, the natural thickener that helps jams to set, so this iced yoghurt has a good deal of body.

1 Put the plums in a nonreactive medium saucepan and add the sugar, cardamom, cinnamon, and cloves. Cook over a medium heat, stirring often, until the plums are very soft, about 10 minutes. Strain through a medium sieve into a large bowl, pressing through as much of the fruit as you can. Discard the plum skins and any stringy fibres. Stir in the lemon juice. Cover and refrigerate for 2 hours, or until cold.

2 Whisk the yoghurt into the chilled spiced plum purée.

3 Pour into the canister of an ice cream maker and freeze according to the manufacturer's directions. Transfer the frozen yoghurt to a covered container and freeze until it is firm enough to scoop, at least 4 hours or overnight.

INGREDIENTS

450g (1lb) coarsely chopped stoned Santa Rosa plums (about 6–8 plums)

140g (5oz) sugar

1tsp ground cardamom

½tsp ground cinnamon

Pinch of cloves

2tbsp fresh lemon juice

675g (1½lb) creamy vanilla yoghurt, chilled

Makes about 1 litre (2 pints)

Brown Sugar–Pineapple Iced Soya Milk

Here's proof a heart-healthy dessert can be as hedonistic as the next. Soya delivers a remarkably rich ice milk, especially tempting when paired with caramel-like brown sugar and chewy bits of crystallised pineapple.

1 In a large bowl, whisk together the soya milk and brown sugar until the sugar dissolves. Whisk in the vanilla extract to blend. If you have time, cover and refrigerate for 1–2 hours to allow the flavours to develop.

2 Pour into the canister of an ice cream maker and freeze according to the manufacturer's directions. Add the crystallised pineapple and process for 1 minute longer. Transfer the iced soya milk to a covered container and freeze until firm enough to scoop, at least 3 hours or overnight.

INGREDIENTS

900ml (1¾ pints) cold soya milk
225g (8oz) dark brown sugar
1½tsp vanilla extract
175g (6oz) coarsely chopped crystallised pineapple rings

Makes about 1¼ litres (2½ pints)

Rhubarb-Raspberry Frozen Yoghurt

An old cook's maxim advises pairing fruits that come into season at the same time, so the combination of these two makes perfect sense. The result is a wonderful frozen dessert that is delightfully tart, sweet, and intense.

1 In a nonreactive medium saucepan, combine the rhubarb, sugar, and water. Cook over a medium heat for about 7 minutes, stirring frequently, until the rhubarb is soft. Set aside for 10 minutes to cool slightly.

2 In a food processor, purée the rhubarb until smooth. Scrape into a large bowl and stir in the yoghurt, raspberries, golden syrup, and orange extract. Cover and refrigerate for 2 hours, or until cold.

3 Pour the yoghurt into the canister of an ice cream maker and freeze according to the manufacturer's directions. Transfer the frozen yoghurt to a covered container and freeze until it is firm enough to scoop, at least 4 hours or overnight.

INGREDIENTS

450g (1lb) sliced fresh rhubarb or thawed frozen rhubarb

175g (6oz) sugar

115ml (4fl oz) water

450g (1lb) plain yoghurt

115g (4oz) fresh or thawed frozen raspberries

1tbsp golden syrup

½tsp orange extract

Makes about 1¼ litres (2½ pints)

Black Forest Frozen Yoghurt

Just like the cake, Black Forest here indicates cherries and chocolate. The combination creates a smashing flavour that makes an indulgent frozen yoghurt.

1 If using fresh cherries, remove any stems. Rinse well and pat dry with kitchen paper. Working over a bowl to catch the juices, cut the cherries in half with a small, sharp stainless steel knife. Cut out the stone with the tip of the knife and drop the cherries into the bowl.

2 Add the sugar to the cherries and toss to mix well. Stir in the yoghurt, lemon juice, and almond extract. Stir to dissolve the sugar. If you have time, cover and refrigerate for 1–2 hours to allow the flavours to develop.

3 Pour the yoghurt base into the canister of an ice cream maker and freeze according to the manufacturer's directions. Add the chocolate and process for 1 minute longer, or until incorporated. Transfer the frozen yoghurt to a covered container and freeze until it is firm enough to scoop, at least 4 hours or overnight.

INGREDIENTS

350g (12oz) fresh sweet cherries or frozen unsweetened Bing cherries, thawed

140g (5oz) sugar

675g (1½lb) vanilla yoghurt

1tbsp fresh lemon juice

¼tsp almond extract

85g (3oz) plain dark chocolate chunks, coarsely chopped and chilled

Makes about 1¼ litres (2½ pints)

Rocky Road Frozen Yoghurt

In frozen desserts, the mix of chocolate, marshmallows, and walnuts has long been dubbed "rocky road." No matter the name, it's a voluptuous combo that appeals to both young and old alike.

1 Preheat the oven to 160°C (325°F/Gas 3). Spread out the walnuts in a small baking pan and toast in the oven until fragrant and very lightly browned, 7–10 minutes. Transfer to a plate and let cool, then coarsely chop.

2 In a medium bowl, combine the yoghurt, sugar, cocoa powder, vanilla extract, and salt. Stir to dissolve the sugar. If you have time, cover and refrigerate for 1–2 hours to allow the flavours to develop.

3 Pour the yoghurt base into the canister of an ice cream maker and freeze according to the manufacturer's directions. Add the chopped toasted walnuts and the marshmallows and process for 1 minute longer, or until incorporated. Transfer the frozen yoghurt to a covered container and freeze until it is firm enough to scoop, at least 3 hours or overnight.

INGREDIENTS

85g (3oz) walnut pieces

900g (2lb) plain yoghurt

225g (8oz) sugar

60g (2oz) unsweetened cocoa powder

1½tsp vanilla extract

Pinch of salt

45g (1½oz) miniature marshmallows

Makes about 1½ litres (3 pints)

COOL TIPS FOR SUCCESS

Finished ice cream benefits from a few hours in the freezer to "ripen." During this time the ice cream becomes firm enough to scoop, and the flavours develop further.

Iced Mocha–Chocolate Chip Soya Milk

Dairy free and delightful, this chocolate- and coffee-flavoured frozen yoghurt laced with chocolate chips could fool anyone into thinking it's a decadent dessert. For proper texture, be sure the tofu you purchase is "silken," the softest kind.

1 In a heavy medium saucepan, combine the chocolate soya milk, sugar, espresso powder, and salt. Bring to the simmer over a medium heat, stirring, until the sugar dissolves and the liquid is hot, about 5 minutes. Remove from the heat and whisk in the cocoa powder until well-blended. Add the chopped chocolate and stir until melted and smooth.

2 In a food processor or blender, purée the tofu until smooth. With the machine running, slowly pour in the warm chocolate mixture. Transfer to a bowl, cover, and refrigerate until cold, at least 4 hours. Whisk in the vanilla extract.

3 Pour the mocha base into the canister of an ice cream maker and freeze according to the manufacturer's directions. Add the chocolate chips and process for 30 seconds to 1 minute longer, or until incorporated. Transfer the iced soya milk to a covered container and freeze until firm enough to scoop, at least 3 hours or overnight.

INGREDIENTS

360ml (12fl oz) chocolate soya milk

225g (8oz) sugar

1½tsp instant espresso powder

Pinch of salt

2tbsp unsweetened cocoa powder

60g (2oz) plain dark chocolate, finely chopped

450g (1lb) silken tofu

1tsp vanilla extract

125g (4½oz) chocolate chips, chilled

Makes about 1 litre (2 pints)

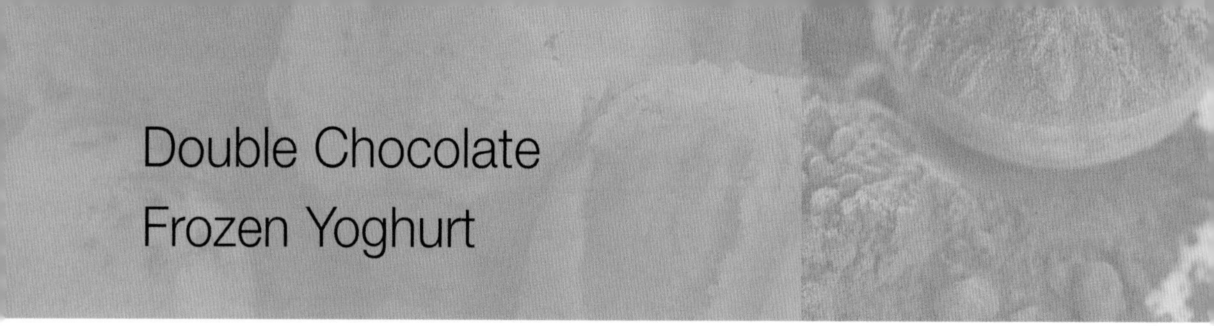

Double Chocolate Frozen Yoghurt

As lovers of some of the better brands of frozen yoghurt know, you can feel virtuous and still have a rollicking good time with flavours like this one.

1 In a medium bowl, combine the yoghurt, sugar, cocoa powder, vanilla extract, and salt. Stir to dissolve the sugar. If you have time, cover and refrigerate for 1–2 hours to allow the flavours to develop.

2 Pour the yoghurt base into the canister of an ice cream maker and freeze according to the manufacturer's directions. Add the chocolate chips and process for 1 minute longer, or until incorporated. Transfer the frozen yoghurt to a covered container and freeze until it is firm enough to scoop, at least 4 hours or overnight.

INGREDIENTS

675g (1½lb) plain yoghurt

175g (6oz) sugar

6tbsp unsweetened cocoa powder

1tsp vanilla extract

Pinch of salt

125g (4½oz) plain dark chocolate chips or chopped plain dark chocolate, chilled

Makes about 1 litre (2 pints)

Quick Cinnamon–Nut Crunch Frozen Yoghurt

Everyone needs a few "quick fix" recipes for days when time is short and demands are high. Vietnamese or other best-quality ground cinnamon magically transforms store-bought vanilla frozen yoghurt into an exotic flavour all your own. For added decadence, chopped chocolate-covered toffee and nuts do the trick. How quick is that?

INGREDIENTS

1 litre (2 pints) vanilla frozen yoghurt

2tbsp ground cinnamon

140g (5oz) coarsely chopped chocolate-covered toffee, chilled

30g (10oz) chopped nuts

Makes about 1 litre (2 pints)

1 Let the frozen yoghurt soften slightly at room temperature for 10–15 minutes—it should be malleable but not liquid. Use a heavy rubber spatula or large wooden spoon to mix in the cinnamon until well-blended. Working quickly, fold in the toffee and nuts.

2 Scrape the frozen yoghurt back into the carton and cover with cling film, pressing against the surface to prevent air pockets. Freeze until firm, at least 6 hours or up to 2 weeks.

COOL TIPS FOR SUCCESS

Store ice cream in the coldest part of the freezer—not in the door. If the original packaging of store-bought ice cream does not appear airtight, enclose the container in a large freezer-safe ziplock plastic bag.

"you never really know your friends
from your enemies
until the ice breaks."

–old Eskimo proverb

sorbets,
granitas,
& ices

Apricot Sorbet

Because apricot season is so painfully brief, and ripe fresh apricots are hard to come by in many regions, this recipe makes it easy by preparing the sorbet with canned. And because the fruit has already been packed in syrup, there's no need to make a simple syrup and let it cool first, which makes this a quick and easy dessert.

1 Drain the apricots, reserving 115ml (4fl oz) of the syrup.

2 In a food processor or blender, purée the apricots until smooth. Transfer to a large bowl. Whisk in the reserved apricot syrup, the sugar, lemon juice, golden syrup, and apricot brandy. Cover and refrigerate for 2 hours, or until the sugar is dissolved and the mixture is very cold.

3 Whisk to blend and pour into the canister of an ice cream maker. Freeze according to the manufacturer's directions. Transfer the sorbet to a covered container and freeze until it is firm enough to scoop, at least 3 hours or overnight.

INGREDIENTS

4 cans (227g or 8oz each) apricot halves in syrup

175g (6oz) sugar

1tbsp fresh lemon juice

1tbsp golden syrup

1tbsp apricot brandy, plain brandy, or amaretto

Makes about 700ml (1½ pints)

Almost-Instant Apple Ice

Quick and convenient, here's an ice that's poured immediately into the ice cream maker. Enjoy as a slush when it comes out of the machine, or as an ice as soon as it firms up in the freezer.

1 In a large bowl, combine the cold apple juice, the apple juice concentrate, lemon juice, Calvados, and golden syrup. Whisk to blend.

2 Pour into the canister of an ice cream maker and freeze according to the manufacturer's directions. Eat at once, while still somewhat slushy, or transfer to a covered container and freeze for at least 2 hours, until firm.

INGREDIENTS

750ml (1½ pints) unsweetened apple juice, well-chilled

175g (6oz) cold applesauce

2tbsp fresh lemon juice

1tbsp Calvados, applejack, or brandy

1tbsp golden syrup

Makes about 1 litre (2 pints)

Green Apple Sorbet

Subtle yet distinctive and traditional in France, this mildly tart sorbet is an excellent dessert to serve after a substantial meal. Garnish with a few very thin slices of unpeeled green apple and douse each dish, if you like, with an extra splash of Calvados.

INGREDIENTS

360ml (12fl oz) unsweetened apple juice

115g (4oz) sugar

1 cinnamon stick

3 large tart green apples, such as Granny Smith, about 675g (1½lb)

3tbsp fresh lemon juice

Pinch of salt

2tbsp Calvados, applejack, apple brandy, or green apple liqueur

Makes about 1 litre (2 pints)

1 In a small saucepan, combine the apple juice, sugar, and cinnamon stick. Cook over a medium heat, stirring often, until the sugar dissolves. Boil the syrup without stirring for 2 minutes. Remove from the heat, cover, and let stand at room temperature for 1 hour so that the syrup cools slowly and absorbs the cinnamon flavour.

2 Peel and core the apples and cut them into eighths. Place in a medium saucepan with the lemon juice, salt, and just enough water to cover. Cook over a medium heat until the apples are soft, about 10 minutes; drain. Transfer the cooked apples to a food processor and purée until the applesauce is smooth.

3 Discard the cinnamon stick from the syrup. Whisk the cinnamon syrup and the Calvados into the applesauce. Transfer to a covered container and refrigerate for 2 hours, or until very cold.

4 Whisk to blend and pour into the canister of an ice cream maker. Freeze according to the manufacturer's directions. Transfer the sorbet to a covered container and freeze until firm enough to scoop, at least 3 hours or overnight.

Meyer Lemon Sorbet

Meyer lemon plants are available from specialist nurseries. This mild citrus fruit is a cross between a lemon and a mandarin and not as acidic as an ordinary lemon. If Meyer lemons are unavailable, you can use any common lemon and substitute fresh orange juice for about 2tbsp of the lemon juice to mellow the acidity.

1 Combine the sugar and water in a small saucepan. Cook over a medium heat, stirring often, until the sugar dissolves. Boil the syrup without stirring for 2 minutes. Remove from the heat and let cool to room temperature.

2 Stir in the lemon juice, lemon rind, golden syrup, and vodka. Cover and refrigerate for 1–2 hours, or until very cold.

3 Pour into the canister of an ice cream maker. Freeze according to the manufacturer's directions. Transfer the sorbet to a covered container and freeze until it is firm enough to scoop, at least 3 hours or overnight.

INGREDIENTS

225g (8oz) sugar

240ml (8fl oz) water

240ml (8fl oz) Meyer lemon juice (from 6–8 lemons)

2tsp finely grated lemon rind

2tbsp golden syrup

1tbsp lemon-flavoured vodka, limoncello, or plain vodka

Makes about 700ml (1½ pints)

Grapefruit Sorbet
with Campari and Mint

Campari is an Italian liqueur that contributes both flavour and colour to this sophisticated ice. Balance is key here, so do not be tempted to add any additional liqueur, or the sorbet may turn bitter.

1 In a large bowl, combine the grapefruit juice, sugar, Campari, golden syrup, and grenadine. Whisk to blend. Cover and refrigerate for 2 hours, or until very cold.

2 Pour into the canister of an ice cream maker and freeze according to the manufacturer's directions. Transfer the sorbet to a covered container and freeze until it is firm enough to scoop, at least 3 hours or overnight.

3 To serve, scoop the sorbet into chilled stemmed glasses or bowls. Drizzle about 1½tbsp Campari-Mint Syrup over each serving and garnish with a mint sprig. Serve at once.

Campari-Mint Syrup

1 In a small saucepan, combine the sugar, water, and mint sprig. Bring to the boil over a medium heat, stirring to dissolve the sugar. Reduce the heat to medium-low and simmer for 10 minutes without stirring. Cover and remove from the heat. Let cool to room temperature.

2 Strain the mint syrup into a bowl. Discard the mint sprig. Stir 3tbsp of the Campari into the syrup. Taste and add more Campari if needed. Cover and refrigerate for 2 hours, or until very cold. Just before serving, stir in the shredded mint.

INGREDIENTS

500ml (16fl oz) pink or Ruby Red grapefruit juice, preferably fresh

225g (8oz) sugar

1tbsp Campari or vodka

1tbsp golden syrup

1–2tsp grenadine, to taste

140ml (5fl oz) Campari-Mint Syrup (recipe follows)

Fresh mint sprigs, for garnish

Makes about 700ml (1½ pints)

Campari-Mint Syrup

115g (4oz) sugar

120ml (4fl oz) water

1 large sprig of mint, plus 1tbsp shredded fresh mint leaves

3–4tbsp Campari

Makes about 140ml (5fl oz)

Honey-Melon Granita

Even though melon is a mild fruit, when it's perfectly ripe and full of flavour, it makes a delicious frozen dessert. Because the melon contains so much water, no syrup is needed. Honey acts as a sweetener and contributes body to the ice.

INGREDIENTS

2kg (4½lb) very ripe cantaloupe or other sweet, fragrant melon, rind removed, deseeded and cubed

180ml (6fl oz) honey

3tbsp fresh lemon or lime juice

Pinch of salt

Makes about 1 litre (2 pints)

1 Working in batches if necessary, purée the melon in a food processor until smooth. With the machine running, add the honey, lemon juice, and salt. Transfer the melon purée to a bowl, cover, and refrigerate for 2 hours, or until very cold.

2 Pour into a shallow 20–28cm (8–9in) square metal baking pan and cover with cling film. Freeze for 45 minutes, or until the granita is frozen around the edges and the surface is covered with a thin layer of ice. Using a fork, break up the ice, scraping the crystals from the edges of the pan and mixing them into the centre to distribute evenly.

3 Return the pan, covered, to the freezer for about 30 minutes, or until the edges have frozen again. Repeat the process at least 3 more times, scraping, mixing, and re-freezing until large, granular ice crystals have formed and the mixture is light and slightly slushy. Do not let the granita harden into a solid mass. Serve at once, or cover and freeze for up to 4 hours.

VARIATION

Honey-Melon Ice: Refrigerate the honey-melon purée until cold. Whisk to blend and pour into the canister of an ice cream maker. Freeze according to the manufacturer's directions, until the mixture is frozen and spoonable but not hard or crumbly. Serve at once, or transfer to a covered container and freeze for at least 30 minutes before serving.

Pear Sorbet with Cabernet Syrup and Fresh Basil

Canned pears make a remarkably fresh-tasting instant sorbet—with no peeling and no poaching.

1 In a food processor or blender, purée the pears until smooth. Transfer to a large bowl.

2 Whisk in 240ml (8fl oz) of the Cabernet Syrup, the lemon juice, and golden syrup. Cover and refrigerate for 2 hours, or until very cold.

3 Stir in the chopped basil and pour into the canister of an ice cream maker. Freeze according to the manufacturer's directions. Transfer the sorbet to a covered container and freeze until it is firm enough to scoop, at least 3 hours or overnight.

4 To serve, scoop the sorbet into chilled stemmed glasses or bowls. Drizzle 1–2tbsp of the remaining Cabernet Syrup over each serving and garnish with a small sprig of basil. Serve at once.

Cabernet Syrup

1 In a nonreactive small saucepan, combine the wine, sugar, basil leaves, and lemon rind. Bring to the boil over a medium heat, stirring to dissolve the sugar. Reduce the heat to medium-low and simmer for 10 minutes without stirring. Cover and remove from the heat. Let cool to room temperature.

2 Strain the wine syrup to remove the basil and lemon. Cover and refrigerate for 2 hours, or until cold.

INGREDIENTS

1 can (410g) pear halves, drained and sliced

550ml (18fl oz) Cabernet Syrup (recipe follows)

1tbsp fresh lemon juice

1tbsp golden syrup

5 fresh basil leaves, finely chopped

Small sprigs of basil, for garnish

Makes about 1 litre (2 pints)

Cabernet Syrup

550ml (18fl oz) Cabernet Sauvignon, or other dry red wine

175g (6oz) sugar

4 large fresh basil leaves

1 strip of lemon rind, 5x4cm (2x1½in)

Makes about 550ml (18fl oz)

Mango-Pineapple Sorbet

Fresh tropical fruits naturally impart plenty of body to this lush sorbet, so there is no need to make a sugar syrup first. The sugar dissolves during the initial chilling time in the refrigerator. Ripe pineapples are not only easy to find these days, you can buy a whole fruit or just the amount you need already cut into chunks in the produce or refrigerated section of your supermarket.

1 Peel the mangoes and cut the fruit away from the large flat stone. In a food processor or blender, purée the mango until smooth. There should be about 750ml (1½ pints) of purée.

2 Transfer to a large bowl. Stir in the chopped pineapple, sugar, lime juice, and rum. Cover and refrigerate until very cold, at least 2 hours or as long as 2 days.

3 Stir the mixture to blend and pour into the canister of an ice cream maker. Freeze according to the manufacturer's directions. Transfer the sorbet to a covered container and freeze until it is firm enough to scoop, at least 3 hours or overnight.

INGREDIENTS

3 ripe large mangoes, about 1kg (2¼lb) total

175g (6oz) finely chopped fresh pineapple

140g (5oz) sugar

3tbsp fresh lime juice

1tbsp light rum or vodka

Makes about 1 litre (2 pints)

Mojito Sorbet

Here's the hottest drink on the bar circuit transformed into a spoonable dessert. Garnish with sprigs of fresh mint or thin slices of lime bent into a twist.

1   In a small saucepan, combine the sugar, water, and mint sprigs. Cook over a medium heat, stirring often, until the sugar dissolves. Boil the syrup without stirring for 2 minutes. Remove from the heat, cover, and let steep at room temperature for 30 minutes.

2   Sieve the mint syrup into a bowl and discard the mint sprigs. Stir in the lime juice, lime rind, rum, and golden syrup. Cover and refrigerate for 2 hours, or until very cold.

3   Pour the mojito base into the canister of an ice cream maker and freeze according to the manufacturer's directions. Add the chopped mint leaves and process for 1 minute longer. Transfer the sorbet to a covered container and freeze until it is firm enough to scoop, at least 3 hours or overnight.

INGREDIENTS

225g (8oz) sugar

500ml (16fl oz) water

5 large sprigs of fresh mint plus 1½tbsp chopped mint leaves

240ml (8fl oz) fresh lime juice

1tsp finely grated lime rind

2tbsp light rum

1tbsp golden syrup

Makes about 700ml (1½ pints)

Gin & Tonic Ice with Lime

Because of the amount of alcohol in this adult dessert, it never freezes as solid as an ordinary ice. Think of it as a frozen cocktail and serve with both a spoon and a straw.

1 In a large bowl, combine the sugar, gin, lime juice, and lime rind. Stir to blend and dissolve the sugar. Cover and refrigerate for 30 minutes, or until very cold.

2 Gradually stir in the tonic water. Pour into the canister of an ice cream maker and freeze according to the manufacturer's directions.

3 Scrape the slush into tall, chilled glasses and garnish the edge of each glass with a slice of lime. Serve at once, with a long-handled tea spoon and a long straw.

INGREDIENTS

175g (6oz) sugar

5tbsp gin

4tbsp fresh lime juice

1tbsp finely grated lime rind

900ml (1¾ pints)
tonic water, chilled

Lime slices, for garnish

Makes about 1¼ litres
(2½ pints)

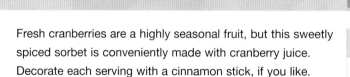

Spiced Cranberry Sorbet

Fresh cranberries are a highly seasonal fruit, but this sweetly spiced sorbet is conveniently made with cranberry juice. Decorate each serving with a cinnamon stick, if you like.

1 In a small saucepan, combine the sugar, water, cinnamon stick, and cloves. Cook over a medium heat, stirring often, until the sugar dissolves. Boil the syrup without stirring for 1 minute. Reduce the heat to low and simmer for 2 minutes longer. Remove the pan from the heat, cover, and let steep at room temperature for 30 minutes.

2 Sieve the syrup into a large heatproof bowl and discard the cinnamon stick and cloves. Stir in the cranberry juice, vodka, and golden syrup. Cover and refrigerate for 2 hours, or until very cold.

3 Whisk to blend and pour into the canister of an ice cream maker. Freeze according to the manufacturer's directions. Transfer to a covered container and freeze until firm enough to scoop, at least 3 hours or overnight.

INGREDIENTS

350g (12oz) sugar

360ml (12fl oz) water

1 cinnamon stick

1 or 2 whole cloves

600ml (1¼ pints) cranberry juice

1tbsp orange- or cranberry-flavoured vodka, or plain vodka

1tbsp golden syrup

Makes about 1 litre (2 pints)

Bellini Sorbet

If you are lucky enough to come upon local peaches that are exceptionally sweet, reduce the sugar by a couple of tablespoons. Otherwise, keep in mind if you taste the peach base before freezing that the cold will diminish the effect of the sugar.

1 In a food processor or blender, purée the peaches with the cold water until smooth. Pour into a large bowl.

2 Stir in the sugar, lemon juice, peach brandy, and golden syrup. If you have time, cover and refrigerate the peach purée for 1–2 hours to allow the flavours to develop.

3 Whisk the purée to blend. Pour into the canister of an ice cream maker and freeze according to the manufacturer's directions. Transfer the sorbet to a covered container and freeze until it is firm enough to scoop, at least 3 hours or overnight.

4 To serve, scoop the sorbet into 4–6 chilled, wide-mouthed champagne coupes or wine glasses. Pour some of the sparkling wine over each and serve at once. Note: A "split" (375 ml) of sparkling wine will be plenty for this recipe. Prosecco, which is traditional for a Bellini, only comes in larger bottles. A good solution: drink all that's left over.

INGREDIENTS

675g (1½lb, about 4–6 medium) ripe peaches, peeled and stoned

4tbsp cold water

225g (8oz) sugar

1tbsp fresh lemon juice

1tbsp peach brandy or vodka

1tbsp golden syrup

1 750ml bottle Prosecco or other dry but fruity sparkling wine, well chilled

Makes about 750ml (1½ pints)

COOL TIPS FOR SUCCESS

Chilling the ice cream base in the refrigerator prior to freezing allows time for the flavours to blend, shortens the processing time in your ice cream machine, and improves the texture of the finished product.

Spirited Pomegranate Sorbet

The popular sweet-tart fruit is here transformed into a fabulous ice, perfect to serve as a dessert or as a palate cleanser between courses at a long meal. Or pack it into a tall glass and add a straw.

1 In a small saucepan, combine the sugar and water. Cook over a medium heat, stirring often, until the sugar dissolves. Boil the syrup without stirring for 3 minutes, or until reduced by half.

2 Pour the sugar syrup into a heatproof medium bowl. Stir in the pomegranate juice, orange juice, gin, golden syrup, and salt. Cover and refrigerate for 3 hours, or until very cold.

3 Pour the pomegranate base into the canister of an ice cream maker and freeze according to the manufacturer's directions. Transfer the sorbet to a covered container and freeze until it is firm enough to scoop, at least 3 hours or overnight. To serve, scoop the sorbet into 4–6 chilled, wide-mouthed champagne coupes, wine glasses, or dessert dishes. Sprinkle the pomegranate seeds on top.

INGREDIENTS

225g (8oz) sugar

180ml (6fl oz) water

500ml (16fl oz) unsweetened pomegranate juice

1½tbsp fresh orange or lemon juice

1½tbsp gin or vodka

1tbsp golden syrup

Pinch of salt

Seeds of 1 fresh pomegranate, for garnish (optional)

Makes about 700ml (1½ pints)

Watermelon-Raspberry Sorbet

Make this in the heat of summer, when fruits are inexpensive and laden with sweet juices. Plain watermelon sorbets often look a bit anaemic, but a small infusion of raspberry intensifies both the appearance and flavour. Pressing the fruits through a sieve ensures a smooth texture. Garnish each serving with a few fresh raspberries or watermelon chunks, if you like.

1 Combine the sugar and water in a small saucepan. Cook over a medium heat, stirring often, until the sugar dissolves. Boil the syrup without stirring for 2 minutes. Remove from the heat and let cool.

2 In a blender or food processor, combine the watermelon chunks, raspberries, lemon juice, vodka, and salt. Pour in the sugar syrup and purée until smooth.

3 Sieve the watermelon purée into a bowl, pressing through as much of the fruit solids as possible. Cover and refrigerate the purée until very cold, at least 2 hours or as long as 2 days.

4 Stir the mixture to blend and pour into the canister of an ice cream maker. Freeze according to the manufacturer's directions. Transfer the sorbet to a covered container and freeze until firm enough to scoop, at least 3 hours or overnight.

INGREDIENTS

175g (6oz) sugar

240ml (8fl oz) water

1kg (2½lb) watermelon, rind and seeds discarded, flesh cut into chunks

60g (2oz) fresh raspberries

1½tbsp fresh lemon juice

1tbsp raspberry vodka or plain vodka

Pinch of salt

Makes about 1 litre (2 pints)

Blood Orange–Ginger Sorbet

This citrus-based sorbet can be made with Valencia or navel oranges, of course, but you shouldn't miss out on the vibrant jolt of colour when blood oranges are available. In addition, the undercurrent of ginger adds a zesty bite to the sweet ice.

1 Combine the sugar, water, ginger, and orange zest in a small saucepan. Cook over a medium heat, stirring often, until the sugar dissolves. Boil the syrup without stirring for 2 minutes. Remove from the heat, cover, and let steep at room temperature for 30 minutes.

2 Sieve the syrup into a bowl and discard the ginger and orange rind. Stir in the orange juice, golden syrup, and vodka. Cover and refrigerate for 2 hours, or until very cold.

3 Pour into the canister of an ice cream maker. Freeze according to the manufacturer's directions. Transfer to a covered container and freeze until firm, at least 3 hours or overnight.

INGREDIENTS

225g (8oz) sugar

240ml (8fl oz) water

45g (1½oz) peeled and coarsely chopped fresh ginger

3 strips of blood orange rind, each about 1x5cm (½x2in)

240ml (8fl oz) blood orange juice (from 4–5 blood oranges)

3tbsp golden syrup

1tbsp orange-flavoured vodka, plain vodka, or orange liqueur

Makes about 700ml (1½ pints)

Mocha Midnight Sorbet

Since this dark sorbet is made exclusively with cocoa powder and contains no solid chocolate, there is very little fat in the form of cocoa butter and no added fat at all in this immensely satisfying dessert. Dark with a distinct illusion of richness, this sorbet will surely satisfy any chocolate lover.

1 In a medium saucepan, combine the sugar, cocoa powder, and salt. Whisk to blend. Gradually mix in the water and espresso or coffee. Whisk in the golden syrup until well-blended.

2 Cook over a medium heat, whisking frequently, for 3–5 minutes, or until the sugar dissolves and the liquid is smooth. Remove from the heat and set aside to cool to room temperature. Stir in the vanilla extract, cover, and refrigerate for 2 hours, or until cold.

3 Whisk briefly to blend, then pour into the canister of an ice cream maker and freeze according to the manufacturer's directions. Transfer the sorbet to a covered container and freeze until it is firm enough to scoop, at least 3 hours or overnight.

INGREDIENTS

350g (12oz) sugar

85g (3oz) unsweetened cocoa powder

⅛tsp salt

360ml (16fl oz) water

240ml (8fl oz) brewed espresso or strong coffee

1tbsp golden syrup

½tsp vanilla extract

Makes about 1 litre (2 pints)

Chocolate Granita

This excellent chocolate ice requires no machine, just a little extra time.

1 In a medium saucepan, combine the sugar, water, and cocoa powder. Cook over a medium heat, whisking, until the sugar dissolves and the mixture is well-blended. Transfer to a bowl and let cool to room temperature. Stir in the chocolate syrup, cover, and refrigerate until very cold, at least 2 hours.

2 Pour the chocolate syrup into a shallow 20–23cm (8–9in) square metal baking pan and cover with cling film. Freeze for 45 minutes, or until the granita is frozen around the edges and the surface is covered with a thin layer of ice. Using a fork, break up the ice, scraping the ice crystals from the edges of the pan and mixing them into the centre to distribute evenly.

3 Return the pan, covered, to the freezer for about 30 minutes, or until the edges have frozen again. Repeat the process at least 3 more times, scraping, mixing, and re-freezing until large, granular ice crystals have formed and the mixture is light and slightly slushy. Do not let the granita harden into a solid mass. Serve at once or cover and freeze for up to 4 hours.

INGREDIENTS

115g (4oz) sugar

750ml (1½ pints) water

1tbsp unsweetened cocoa powder

75ml (2½fl oz) Chocolate Syrup, home-made (page 179) or store-bought

Makes about 900ml (1¾ pints)

VARIATION

Chocolate Ice: Prepare the chocolate syrup as in Step 1 and refrigerate until cold. Whisk to blend and pour into the canister of an ice cream maker. Freeze according to the manufacturer's directions, until the mixture is frozen and spoonable, but not hard or crumbly. Serve at once, or transfer to a covered container and freeze for about 30 minutes before serving.

Espresso Granita

That espresso is the most classic of granita flavours should come as no surprise, since the coarse-crystalled ice originated in Italy. It's a frozen dessert you can make with no machine, and the effect is appreciably different from a standard sorbet. Serve with biscotti or amaretti.

INGREDIENTS

500ml (16fl oz) freshly brewed espresso or very strong coffee

4tbsp sugar

Makes about 700ml (1½ pints)

1 In a medium bowl, combine the hot espresso and sugar. Stir to dissolve the sugar. Let cool to room temperature. Cover and refrigerate until very cold, at least 2 hours.

2 Pour into a shallow 20cm (8in) square pan and cover with cling film. Freeze for 45 minutes, or until the granita is frozen around the edges and the surface is covered with a thin layer of ice. Using a fork, break up the ice, scraping the ice crystals from the edges of the pan and mixing them into the centre to distribute evenly.

3 Return the pan, covered, to the freezer for about 30 minutes, or until the edges have frozen again. Repeat the process at least 3 more times, scraping, mixing, and re-freezing until large, granular ice crystals have formed and the mixture is light and slightly slushy. Do not let the granita harden into a solid mass. Serve at once, or cover and freeze for up to 4 hours.

VARIATIONS

Café Latte Granita: Add 240ml (8fl oz) of milk to the espresso mixture in Step 1.

Espresso Ice: Here's the same base processed in an ice cream maker. Refrigerate the espresso mixture until cold, as directed in Step 1. Pour into the canister of an ice cream maker. Freeze according to the manufacturer's directions, until the mixture is frozen and spoonable. Serve at once or transfer to a covered container and freeze for about 30 minutes before serving.

"a hot fudge sundae and a trashy
novel is my idea
of heaven."

–Barbara Walters

sundaes
& parfaits

Warm Amaretto-Peach Sundae

This is a chic, unstructured sundae that incorporates a classic Italian dessert—baked fresh peaches stuffed with an intense almond filling—with a fresh peach's favourite companion: raspberry sauce. You can make it easy by forming these sundaes with store-bought ice cream.

1 Preheat the oven to 180°C (350°F/Gas 4). Spread out the almonds in an even layer in a small baking pan. Toast in the oven, stirring once or twice, for 7–9 minutes, or until lightly browned and fragrant. Transfer to a dish and set aside to cool. Leave the oven on. Reserve half of the toasted almonds for garnish; finely chop the remainder.

2 Generously grease a 2-litre baking dish with the butter. Cut 1 peach in half through its stem end. Twist the halves in opposite directions to separate and free them from the stone. Repeat with remaining peaches. Place the peach halves, cut-sides up, in the prepared dish and drizzle with 1tbsp of the amaretto.

3 In a medium bowl, combine the chopped almonds with the remaining 1tbsp amaretto, the crushed amaretti, brown sugar, egg yolk, and salt. Mix with a fork until well-blended. Stuff the hollow of each peach with an equal amount of the almond filling, mounding it slightly to resemble a peach stone.

4 Bake for 20–25 minutes, or until the topping is crisp and browned and the peaches are softened, but still hold their shape. Baste the peaches with any juices from the baking dish.

5 To serve, drizzle about 3tbsp of Raspberry Sauce onto each of 6 dessert plates or shallow bowls. Place 1 warm peach half on each. Add 1 or 2 scoops of ice cream on the side, sprinkle the reserved toasted almonds on top, and serve at once.

INGREDIENTS

60g (2oz) flaked almonds

15g (½oz) unsalted butter

3 ripe but firm peaches

2tbsp amaretto liqueur

about 4 large amaretti (crisp Italian almond macaroons)

4tbsp dark brown sugar

1 egg yolk

Pinch of salt

180ml (6fl oz) Raspberry Sauce (page 66)

1 litre (2 pints) Tahitian Double Vanilla Ice Cream (page 12), Fresh Peach Ice Cream (page 14), or 1 litre store-bought vanilla or peach ice cream

Serves 6

Butterscotch-Pecan Sundae

Easy, gooey, and sweet, this classic sundae offers a tempting alternative to hot fudge. Fresh pecans will make all the difference to the sauce.

1 Place a scoop of ice cream in each of 4 tall sundae glasses. Ladle 3–4tbsp of the Butterscotch-Pecan Sauce over the ice cream. Repeat with the remaining ice cream and most of the sauce.

2 Top each sundae with a dollop of whipped cream and garnish with a few pecan pieces from the sauce.

Butterscotch-Pecan Sauce

1 Preheat the oven to 180°C (350°F/Gas 4). Spread out the pecans in a small baking pan. Toast in the oven for 7–10 minutes, stirring once or twice, until lightly browned and fragrant. Transfer to a dish and set aside to cool.

2 In a small saucepan, combine the brown sugar, golden syrup, cream, butter, and salt. Bring to the boil over a medium heat, stirring frequently. Reduce the heat to medium-low and cook for 10–15 minutes longer, or until the sauce has thickened and reduced to about 360ml (12fl oz). Remove from the heat and set aside to cool for about 30 minutes. Stir in the vanilla extract and the toasted pecans. Cover and refrigerate for up to 1 week. Serve at room temperature or barely warm.

> **VARIATION**
>
> **Butterscotch Sauce:** For plain butterscotch sauce, simply omit the pecans and skip to Step 2.

INGREDIENTS

750ml (1½ pints) No-Cook Vanilla Ice Cream (page 25) or store-bought vanilla ice cream

Butterscotch-Pecan Sauce (recipe follows)

Whipped cream, for garnish

Makes 4

Butterscotch-Pecan Sauce

60g (2oz) pecan halves and pieces

225g (8oz) light brown sugar

120ml (4fl oz) golden syrup

120ml (4fl oz) double cream

60g (2oz) unsalted butter, cut into pieces

Pinch of salt

1tsp vanilla extract

Makes about 350ml (12fl oz)

Peach Melba Coupe

Peach Melba is a classic ice cream dessert served in stemmed glasses with wide bowls called coupes. You can also dice the peaches and layer the dessert into tall narrow glasses and call it a parfait. To turn this into an "almost-instant" dessert, simply use canned or frozen peaches and skip Steps 1 and 2.

1 Dip the peaches into a saucepan of boiling water for 10–30 seconds to loosen the skins. Lift out with a slotted spoon and rinse under cold running water. Slip off the skins. Halve the peaches and remove the stones.

2 In a medium saucepan, combine the sugar, water, lemon rind, cinnamon stick, and cloves. Bring to the boil, stirring to dissolve the sugar. Reduce the heat to low and simmer for 5 minutes. Add the peach halves and poach, turning gently once so they cook evenly, until they are barely tender, about 10 minutes. Remove from the heat and let the peaches cool in the syrup, then cover and refrigerate until chilled. (The peaches can be poached up to a day in advance.)

3 Drain the peaches and cut them into slices.

4 To assemble the desserts, choose 4 coupe glasses or tall, narrow, straight-sided parfait dishes. Put a small scoop of vanilla ice cream in the bottom of each glass. Add a layer of peaches, using about half. Drizzle on half the Raspberry Sauce. Repeat with more ice cream and the remaining peaches and raspberry sauce. Top with a small dollop or swirl of whipped cream, if you like, and garnish with whole berries or chopped almonds. Serve at once.

INGREDIENTS

3 ripe peaches

175g (6oz) sugar

240ml (8fl oz) water

1 strip of lemon rind

1 cinnamon stick,
7½cm (3in) long

2 whole cloves

500ml (16fl oz) Tahitian Double Vanilla Ice Cream (page 12) or your favourite premium brand

Raspberry Sauce (page 66)

Sweetened whipped cream, for garnish (optional)

Chopped toasted almonds or whole berries, for garnish

Serves 4

Brandied Fruit Parfait

These parfaits are perfectly suited to holiday entertaining, or to any wintry evening that calls for a festive dessert, because they can be completely assembled a day in advance. If you have extra angelica after making the Fruit Sauce, use a small leaf-shaped cookie cutter to form holly leaves as a garnish for each serving. Otherwise, decorate the parfaits with cinnamon sticks.

1 In a heavy 1-litre nonreactive saucepan, combine the Brandied Fruit Sauce, orange juice, brown sugar, orange rind and juice, bourbon whiskey, and cinnamon. Bring to the boil over a medium heat, stirring to dissolve the sugar. Reduce the heat to medium-low and cook, stirring occasionally, for 5–10 minutes, or until the sauce thickens. Stir in the cream until well-blended.

2 Transfer the sauce into a heatproof bowl and let cool completely. Use at once or cover and refrigerate for up to 4 days.

3 To assemble the parfaits, spoon about 1tbsp of the brandied fruit into the bottom of each of 4 parfait glasses. Add 1 scoop of ice cream to each and top with about 3tbsp of sauce. Repeat with 1 more scoop of ice cream and the remaining sauce. Cover each parfait with cling film and freeze until firm, at least 4 hours or overnight.

4 About 15 minutes before serving, transfer the parfaits from the freezer to the refrigerator to soften slightly. Discard the cling film and top each parfait with whipped cream and a light dusting of nutmeg. Serve at once.

INGREDIENTS

240ml (8fl oz) Brandied Fruit Sauce (page 187), or good quality store-bought all-fruit mincemeat

180ml (6fl oz) orange juice

140g (5oz) dark brown sugar

Finely grated rind and juice from 1 orange

4tbsp bourbon whiskey, brandy, or dark rum

½tsp ground cinnamon

3tbsp double cream

750ml (1½ pints) Cinnamon-Basil Ice Cream (page 18), or store-bought clotted cream, cinnamon, or vanilla ice cream

Whipped cream and freshly-grated nutmeg, for garnish

Serves 4

Frozen Yoghurt Berry Parfait with Cinnamon-Nut Crunch

When cereal is toasted with sweetened nuts, it makes a delicious cinnamon "crunch" similar to granola and ideal for layering in parfaits.

1 In a large frying pan, melt the butter over a medium heat. Add the cereal, sugar, honey, and nuts. Cook, stirring frequently, for 4–5 minutes or until the sugar dissolves and the mixture is lightly toasted and caramelised. Stir in the cinnamon. Spread on a foil-lined baking sheet and set aside to cool completely. Use your fingers to break up the cinnamon-nut crunch into small clusters.

2 To assemble the parfaits, place 1 scoop of frozen yoghurt in the bottom of each of 4 parfait glasses. Top each with 4tbsp of the berries and 4tbsp of the cinnamon-nut crunch. Add another scoop of yoghurt and repeat the layers by adding the remaining berries and ending with a layer of crunch. Serve at once.

INGREDIENTS

15g (½oz) unsalted butter

75g (2½oz) corn or wheat flake cereal, crushed into coarse crumbs

1tbsp sugar

1tbsp honey

60g (2oz) flaked almonds, chopped walnuts, or chopped pecans

1tsp ground cinnamon

1 litre (2 pints) raspberry frozen yoghurt or frozen yoghurt or ice cream flavour of your choice

225g (8oz) assorted fresh berries, such as raspberries, blackberries, blueberries, and sliced strawberries

Serves 4

Roast Banana Split with Mixed Berries

Here's a new twist on an old favourite, the banana split. All the bells and whistles included here were inspired by a roasted banana split sundae served at a California café that was popular in my youth, Rosalie's. While hot banana, baked in its skin, makes for a pleasing contrast to the cold ice cream, plain sliced raw banana is much more attractive. Please note: both sauces should be made before starting to assemble the sundaes.

1 Place 4 dinner-sized plates in the freezer. If desired, scoop out 4 servings each of vanilla and chocolate ice cream and return them to the freezer until serving time.

2 If you choose to roast the bananas, preheat the oven to 180°C (350°F/Gas 4). Place the bananas in their peels on a foil-lined baking sheet. Bake for 15–20 minutes, or until the skins turn black and the fruit is warm throughout. When cool enough to handle, cut each banana in half lengthways and remove the peel. Otherwise, simply peel the raw bananas and split them lengthways in half.

3 To assemble the banana splits, arrange 2 banana halves in each chilled dish. Working quickly, place a scoop of vanilla ice cream on one end of the plate and a scoop of chocolate on the opposite. Pile 60g (2oz) berries in the centre. Drizzle the Toffee Sauce over the vanilla ice cream and the Chocolate-Nut Sauce over the chocolate ice cream. Add a dollop of whipped cream and garnish with a mint sprig. Serve at once.

INGREDIENTS

4 firm but ripe bananas, in their skins

500ml (16fl oz) Tahitian Double Vanilla Ice Cream (page 12), or your favourite premium brand

500ml (16fl oz) Chocolate Custard Ice Cream (page 30), or your favourite premium brand

225g (8oz) fresh berries (raspberries, blackberries, hulled and quartered strawberries, and/or blueberries)

Toffee Sauce (page 185)

Chocolate-Nut Sauce (page 184)

Sweetened whipped cream, for garnish

4 small sprigs of mint, for garnish

Serves 4

Strawberry Sundae

Nothing tastes better than sweet, succulent strawberries served at the height of their picking season. Use the freshest fruit available to make this sundae a real treat.

1 Put 4 scoops of strawberry ice cream in each of 4 tall glasses or serving dishes. Spoon 2tbsp Simple Strawberry Sauce over each. Add another scoop and the remaining sauce.

2 Top the sundaes with a dollop or swirl of whipped cream and garnish with a fresh strawberry.

Simple Strawberry Sauce

1 Working in batches if needed, purée the berries in a food processor or blender until smooth. Transfer to a bowl and stir in the lemon juice and 2tbsp of the sugar. Set aside for 2 or 3 minutes to allow the sugar to dissolve.

2 If you're adding a liqueur, stir it in. Taste the sauce and add the remaining 1tbsp sugar if you think it's needed. Use at once, or cover and refrigerate for up to 2 days.

INGREDIENTS

750ml (1½ pints) Strawberry Dream Light Ice Cream (page 46), or your favourite premium strawberry ice cream

Simple Strawberry Sauce (recipe follows)

Whipped cream, for garnish

4 whole strawberries, for garnish

Makes 4

Simple Strawberry Sauce
450g (1lb) strawberries
2tsp fresh lemon juice
2–3tbsp sugar, to taste
1tbsp Grand Marnier or Framboise (optional)

Makes about 240ml (8fl oz)

Sticky Toffee Sundae

Sticky toffee pudding is one of Britain's greatest contributions to modern culture. In this case, it's a sweet moist date cake topped with toffee. Here, a scoop of ice cream transforms the "pudding" into a fabulous sundae. This dessert is rich, so serve small portions to begin.

1 In a heavy medium saucepan, combine the dates and water. Bring to the boil over a medium heat. Remove from the heat, stir in the bicarbonate of soda, and let stand for about 30 minutes.

2 Preheat the oven to 160°C (325°F/Gas 3). Generously grease a 23cm (9in) square baking pan. Line the bottom with baking parchment.

3 In a large bowl, whisk the butter and brown sugar with an electric mixer for 3–5 minutes, or until light and very fluffy. Add the eggs, one at a time, whisking well after each addition. Beat in the vanilla extract. With a wooden spoon or rubber spatula, mix in the flour and baking powder. Add the date mixture and mix just until well-blended. Turn the batter into the prepared baking pan.

4 Bake the sticky toffee pudding for 40–45 minutes, or until the cake is just beginning to pull away from the sides of the pan and a toothpick inserted into the centre comes out with a moist crumb. Remove the pan from the oven. Using a toothpick, poke holes all over the top of the cake and drizzle with about 180ml (6fl oz) of the warm Vanilla Toffee Sauce. Let cool in the pan on a wire rack for at least 30 minutes before cutting into squares or rectangles. Serve the "pudding" warm or at room temperature.

5 To assemble the dessert, place a portion of sticky toffee pudding on each of 6 or 8 dessert plates or in shallow bowls. Top with a large scoop of ice cream and drizzle warm Vanilla Toffee Sauce over all.

INGREDIENTS

225g (8oz) chopped stoned dates

300ml (1fl oz) water

1tsp bicarbonate of soda

60g (2oz) unsalted butter, softened

175g (6oz) dark brown sugar

2 eggs

1½tsp vanilla extract

200g (7oz) plain flour

1tsp baking powder

750ml (1½ pints) Tahitian Double Vanilla Ice Cream (page 12) or your favourite premium brand

Vanilla Toffee Sauce (page 185)

Serves 6–8

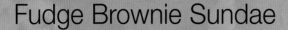

Fudge Brownie Sundae

Rich, fudgy brownies layered with vanilla ice cream and topped off with an intense bittersweet chocolate sauce can go from casual to dressy, depending upon your dishes. Of course, you can always make it easy by simply purchasing the brownies.

1 Preheat the oven to 180°C (350°F/Gas 4). Generously grease a 20cm (8in) square baking pan. Dust with flour; shake out the excess.

2 Place a large heatproof bowl over a pan of barely simmering water. Add the chocolate and butter and cook over a low heat, stirring, until melted and smooth. Remove from the heat and set aside to cool for 5 minutes.

3 Whisk in the sugar. Add the eggs and vanilla extract and whisk until well-mixed. Add the flour and salt and stir until just blended. Turn the batter into the prepared pan.

4 Bake the brownies for 30 minutes, or until a toothpick inserted 5cm (2in) from the edge comes out with small, moist crumbs. Do not overbake. Cool on a wire rack for 20–30 minutes. Cut into 16 squares. Serve at once, or wrap well and refrigerate for up to 3 days; freeze for longer storage.

5 To assemble the sundaes, place 1 brownie square in each of 8 large goblets, tall glasses, or dessert dishes. Top with a scoop of ice cream. Repeat with a second brownie and more ice cream. Drizzle 2 or 3 tablespoons of barely warm Bittersweet Fudge Sauce over each sundae. To complete the picture, top each sundae, if you like, with a dollop of whipped cream and a maraschino cherry. Serve at once.

INGREDIENTS

115g (4oz) very bitter plain dark chocolate, finely chopped

115g (4oz) unsalted butter, cut into pieces

350g (12oz) sugar

3 eggs, lightly beaten

1½tsp vanilla extract

85g (3oz) plain flour

¼tsp salt

1 litre (2 pints) Tahitian Double Vanilla Ice Cream (page 12), or the flavour of your choice

Bittersweet Fudge Sauce (page 184)

Whipped cream and maraschino cherries, for garnish (optional)

Serves 8

Haute Fudge Sundae

There's a reason a recipe becomes a classic. In both flavour and texture, this is simply one of the best combinations of ice cream and sauce ever conceived. For the full effect, the dessert must be served in old-fashioned dessert glasses.

1 Place a scoop of ice cream in each of 4 tall dessert glasses. Ladle 2 or 3tbsp of Haute Fudge Sauce over the ice cream. Repeat with the remaining ice cream and more sauce.

2 Top each sundae with a dollop or swirl of whipped cream and garnish with a sprinkling of chopped walnuts and a single cherry.

Haute Fudge Sauce

1 In a heavy nonreactive medium saucepan, combine the cream, brown sugar, cocoa powder, golden syrup, and salt. Cook over a low heat, whisking often, for 5 minutes, or until the sugar dissolves and bubbles appear on the surface. Remove from the heat.

2 Add the chopped chocolate and the butter to the hot cocoa cream. Whisk until melted and smooth. Stir in the vanilla extract.

3 Use the fudge sauce at once or let cool to room temperature. If made in advance, refrigerate in a covered jar for up to 1 week.

INGREDIENTS

750ml (1½ pints) Tahitian Double Vanilla Ice Cream (page 12), or your favourite premium brand

Haute Fudge Sauce (recipe follows)

Whipped cream, for garnish

30g (1oz) chopped toasted walnuts, for garnish (optional)

4 maraschino cherries, for garnish

Serves 4

Haute Fudge Sauce

120ml (4fl oz) double cream

225g (8oz) dark brown sugar

60g (2oz) unsweetened cocoa powder

4tbsp golden syrup

Pinch of salt

60g (2oz) plain dark chocolate, finely chopped

30g (1oz) unsalted butter, cut into pieces

1tsp vanilla extract

Makes about 350ml (12fl oz)

Candy Cane Sundae with Peppermint Fudge Sauce

It's Christmas in July or ice cream for Christmas, depending upon when you choose to serve these charming sundaes, which will delight a younger crowd. Hard peppermints are a favourite year round, but during the holidays you may want to use the candy canes available in supermarkets and sweet shops.

1 Unwrap all the mints. Place them in a heavy-duty plastic bag and crush into small pieces with a rolling pin or the bottom of a pan. Avoid smashing them into a powder.

2 Place 2 scoops of vanilla ice cream in each of 4 dessert glasses or dishes. Drizzle about 4tbsp of warm Peppermint Fudge Sauce over each serving of ice cream and top with 1tbsp of the crushed peppermints. Serve at once.

Peppermint Fudge Sauce

1 In a heatproof medium bowl, combine the chocolate, butter, water, golden syrup, vanilla extract, peppermint extract, and salt. Set over a pan of barely simmering water and stir constantly until the chocolate and butter are melted and the sauce is smooth.

2 Use the sauce at once, or transfer to a container and let cool; then cover and refrigerate for up to 1 week.

INGREDIENTS

2 peppermint candy canes or 50g (1¾oz) peppermint candies

1 litre (2 pints) Tahitian Double Vanilla Ice Cream (page 12), or your favourite premium brand

Peppermint Fudge Sauce (recipe follows)

Serves 4

Peppermint Fudge Sauce

225g (8oz) plain dark chocolate, chopped

60g (2oz) unsalted butter, cut into pieces

4tbsp water

4tbsp golden syrup

½tsp vanilla extract

¼tsp peppermint extract

Pinch of salt

Makes about 240ml (8fl oz)

Black and White Chocolate Cups

More of a refined dessert than an ice cream sundae, these charming ice cream–filled cups provide the perfect finish for an elegant dinner party.

1 Line 10 muffin tins with paper liners. Place the chocolate in a heatproof bowl placed over a pan of barely simmering water. Cook over a low heat, stirring occasionally, until melted and smooth. Remove the chocolate from the heat and set aside for 5–10 minutes to cool and thicken slightly.

2 Spoon 1tbsp of the melted chocolate into each paper liner. Using a narrow pastry brush, spread the chocolate over the bottom and up the sides of the liners to coat evenly, leaving a 3mm (⅛in) margin at the top. Freeze for 30 minutes or until the chocolate is firm. Set the bowl of chocolate aside.

3 Remove the chocolate cups from the freezer. Return the bowl of chocolate to the pan of barely simmering water. Add 1 more tbsp of warm chocolate to each cup and brush over the bottom and up the sides of the paper liner, forming a second layer, still leaving the bare margin at the top. Refrigerate or freeze for at least 1 hour.

4 To separate the chocolate from each paper liner, grasp the top edges of the paper and gently peel it away from the chocolate; set on a baking parchment-lined baking sheet. Do not rush this process, as the cups are fragile. Refrigerate or freeze until the chocolate is firm; then cover and refrigerate until needed.

5 To serve, carefully set a frozen chocolate cup on each dessert plate. Fill with a scoop of White Chocolate Ice Cream (made without the Bittersweet Fudge Ripple, if desired). Top with a dollop of Chocolate Whipped Cream and garnish with a single berry or crystallised violet.

INGREDIENTS

350g (12oz) plain dark or white chocolate, chopped

1 litre (2 pints) White Chocolate Ice Cream (page 26), Tahitian Double Vanilla Ice Cream (page 12), or your favourite premium brand

Chocolate Whipped Cream (page 185), for garnish

Fresh raspberries or crystallised violets, for garnish

Serves 8–10

Ethereal Coffee Sundae

This sundae uses Blum's Coffee Crunch, a melt-in-your-mouth candy topping, which was originally made by a popular San Francisco bakery.

1 Place a scoop of ice cream in each of 4 tall dessert glasses. Ladle about 2tbsp of the Maple-Bathed Walnuts over the ice cream. Repeat with the remaining ice cream and walnuts.

2 Cap each sundae with a dollop or swirl of whipped cream and sprinkle 1–2tbsp of the Coffee Crunch over all.

Blum's Coffee Crunch

1 Coat a Swiss roll pan or other large baking sheet with mild-flavoured cooking oil, or line with a silicone liner.

2 In a 2–3 litre saucepan, combine the sugar, espresso, and golden syrup. Bring to the simmer over a medium-low heat, stirring to dissolve the sugar. Increase the heat to medium-high and boil without stirring until the syrup reaches 140°C.

3 Remove the pan from the heat and let the boiling subside, then add the bicarbonate of soda. The syrup will bubble up to about 4 times its original volume. Use a long-handled whisk to incorporate the bicarbonate of soda. While it is still hot and liquid, pour onto the prepared Swiss roll pan. Leave the big bubbling mass on the baking sheet—it will shrink a bit as it cools.

4 Let the crunch stand uncovered at room temperature for 30–40 minutes, or until completely cool. Lift it off of the pan and crack into 3 or 4 pieces. Immediately place each chunk in a heavy-duty plastic ziplock bag to prevent it from becoming sticky. Just before serving, crush the crunch into irregular bite-sized chunks.

INGREDIENTS

750ml (1½ pints) Coffee Ice Cream (page 32) or your favourite flavour

Maple-Bathed Walnuts (page 186) or Easy Chocolate Sauce (page 184)

Whipped cream, for garnish

Blum's Coffee Crunch, for garnish (recipe follows)

Makes 4

Blum's Coffee Crunch

350g (12oz) sugar

4tbsp brewed espresso or strong coffee

4tbsp golden syrup

1tbsp bicarbonate of soda, sifted

Makes about 400g (14oz)

Tiramisu Parfait

To form these charming individual desserts, you'll need four freezer-safe glasses (175–250ml or 6–8 ounces each), such as Irish coffee mugs, bistro glasses, or individual soufflé moulds.

1 Combine the sugar and water in a small saucepan. Cook over a medium heat, stirring often, until the sugar dissolves. Boil the syrup without stirring for 2 minutes. Remove from the heat and let cool to room temperature. Stir in the Cognac and coffee.

2 Pour half the coffee syrup into a wide shallow bowl. Add half the sponge fingers and turn them until they have absorbed all of the liquid. Repeat with the remaining syrup and sponge fingers.

3 To assemble the parfaits: Let the ice cream stand at room temperature for 10–15 minutes to soften. Working quickly, arrange alternating layers of ice cream and sponge fingers, trimmed to fit, in the parfait glasses, filling them about ¾ full. Cover tightly and freeze for at least 2 hours and up to 5 days.

4 To serve, remove the parfaits from the freezer about 10 minutes before serving to allow them to soften slightly. Top each with a dollop of whipped cream and a dusting of cocoa powder.

INGREDIENTS

75g (2½oz) sugar

75ml (2½fl oz) water

3tbsp Cognac, brandy, or rum

3tbsp double-strength brewed coffee or 1tbsp instant espresso powder, dissolved in 3tbsp boiling water

10–12 sponge fingers

500ml (16fl oz) Coffee Ice Cream (page 32), or your favourite premium brand

Whipped cream, for garnish

Cocoa powder, for dusting

Serves 4

COOL TIPS FOR SUCCESS

"Flash freezing" composed ice cream desserts will keep your garnishes intact. Simply freeze the completed dessert uncovered until the surface is firm to the touch, then wrap airtight.

"Jacket Potato" Sundae

People are enchanted by whimsical desserts that trick the eye, what the French call *trompe l'oeil*. This pseudo spud is perfect for April Fool's Day or St. Patrick's Day . . . or anytime you want to elicit a smile or two from your guests.

1 Have ready 4 sheets of cling film about 25cm (10in) long. Place 2 or 3 scoops of ice cream side by side on each sheet and enclose in the plastic, wrapping them airtight. Use your hands to squeeze and mould each batch of ice cream into a smooth, irregular oval resembling a large potato. Freeze the 4 "potatoes" for at least 2 hours, or until firm.

2 Place the drinking chocolate powder in a large shallow bowl. Working with one "potato" at a time, unwrap the ice cream. Use the tip of a teaspoon to make a few realistic indentations on the surface, then roll in the chocolate powder to coat completely. Place in a baking pan or a deep plastic container large enough to hold all the "potatoes." Repeat with the remaining ice cream. Insert 5 pine nuts, randomly spaced, into each potato to resemble sprouting eyes. Cover and freeze for at least 2 hours or until firm. Reserve any leftover chocolate powder for touch-ups.

3 If any ice cream is visible on the "potatoes," roll in chocolate powder again to cover. Place 1 "potato" on each of 4 chilled dessert plates. Working quickly, draw a knife lengthways down the centre of each "potato," making an indentation 2–2½cm (¾–1in) deep. Gently press both ends, as if opening a baked potato to expose the inside. Top each with a large dollop of marshmallow fluff (to resemble soured cream). Scatter toffee bits (for bacon bits) over the top and sprinkle with green vermicelli or angelica (for chives). Drizzle chocolate sauce on each plate, or pass at the table. Serve at once.

INGREDIENTS

1 litre (2 pints) Tahitian Double Vanilla Ice Cream (page 12), or your favourite premium brand, softened slightly

115g (4oz) drinking chocolate powder

20 pine nuts (about 1½tsp)

1 jar (213g) marshmallow fluff or 550ml (16fl oz) whipped cream

2tbsp chocolate-covered toffee bits

2tsp green vermicelli or angelica, cut into julienne strips

240–500ml (8–16fl oz) Easy Chocolate Sauce (page 184), or your favourite store-bought chocolate sauce or syrup

Serves 4

"in my films, all the great things are put together. it's not like one kind of ice cream, but rather a very big sundae."

–film director George Lucas

ice cream cakes, moulded desserts, & pies

Baby Baked Alaskas

Great for entertaining, these meringue-cloaked ice cream cakes can be completely assembled a day in advance. The secret of success is to make sure your oven is up to temperature before baking them. That way, the meringue will brown before the ice cream melts.

1 Using a 7½cm (3in) round cookie cutter, stamp out a circle from each slice of cake. Arrange the rounds of cake on a foil-lined baking sheet. Place a generous rounded scoop of ice cream on top of each piece of cake. Freeze for at least 30 minutes.

2 In a large bowl with an electric mixer, whisk the egg whites with the cream of tartar until foamy. Gradually whisk in the sugar 1tbsp at a time. Continue to whisk the meringue until stiff glossy peaks form when the whisk is lifted.

3 Remove the ice cream–topped cakes from the freezer and, working quickly, cover each one with the meringue, spreading it on thickly and making sure to completely enclose the cake and ice cream. Return the cakes to the freezer for at least 1 hour or up to 1 day.

4 When you are ready to serve, preheat the oven to 240°C (475°F/Gas 9). Set the frozen sheet of desserts in the oven and bake for 3–5 minutes, until the edges of the meringue are browned. Serve at once.

INGREDIENTS

6 slices of Madeira cake, cut 1cm (½in) thick

1 litre (2 pints) ice cream, your choice of flavour

4 egg whites

⅛tsp cream of tartar

115g (4oz) caster sugar

Serves 6

Frozen Banana-Ginger Coconut Cream Pie

This is not like any banana cream pie that you've had before, but one taste and you surely won't forget it. Ginger jam and coconut give this lovely dessert another dimension of flavour. Of course, to make it easy, you may substitute a store-bought pastry case.

1 Preheat the oven to 180°C (350°F/Gas 4). Spread out the coconut evenly on a small baking sheet. Toast in the oven, stirring frequently, for 7–10 minutes, or until lightly browned. Transfer to a plate and let cool.

2 In a large bowl, combine the softened ice cream and 45g (1½oz) of the coconut. Using a large wooden spoon or a rubber spatula, stir in the coconut. Working quickly, gently stir in the bananas so they remain in slices and large pieces. Pile half the ice cream into the prepared crust. Dollop teaspoons of the ginger jam randomly over the ice cream and cover with the remaining ice cream, mounding it in the centre. Freeze until completely set, at least 3 hours or for up to 3 days.

3 To serve, let the pie stand in the refrigerator for 10–15 minutes to soften slightly. Meanwhile, in a large chilled bowl with a chilled whisk, whip the double cream with the sugar and vanilla extract until stiff. Spread the whipped cream over the pie. Sprinkle the remaining 15g (½oz) toasted coconut on top. Use a long, sharp knife dipped in hot water and wiped dry to slice the pie into wedges.

INGREDIENTS

60g (2oz) desiccated coconut

1½ litres (3 pints) Tahitian Double Vanilla Ice Cream (page 12), or your favourite premium brand, softened slightly

2 ripe bananas, peeled and sliced

23cm (9in) Digestive Biscuit Crumb Crust (page 185), baked and chilled, or store-bought pastry case

140g (5oz) ginger or apricot jam, chopped if there are any large pieces

240ml (8fl oz) double cream

1tbsp sugar

½tsp vanilla extract

Serves 6–8

Profiteroles

Crisp, golden profiteroles, filled with vanilla ice cream and bathed in chocolate or raspberry sauce is one of the all-time great classic desserts.

1   Preheat the oven to 200°C (400°F/Gas 6). In a heavy large saucepan, combine the butter, water, sugar, and salt. Bring to the boil over a medium heat, stirring to melt the butter. When the water reaches a full boil and the butter is melted, add the flour all at once. Reduce the heat to medium-low and beat vigorously until the dough masses together in a ball, 1–2 minutes. Remove from the heat.

2   Either by hand or with an electric mixer, whisk in the eggs one at a time, making sure that each egg is fully incorporated before adding the next. Continue beating until the dough is very smooth and shiny. (The dough can be mixed in a food processor, but it will not incorporate as much air.)

3   Using 2 spoons or a large pastry bag fitted with a 1cm (½in) wide plain tip, drop 24–30 small mounds of dough (about 2cm or ¾in diameter) about 4cm (1½in) apart on a greased baking sheet.

4   Bake for 20 minutes. Reduce the oven temperature to 190°C (375°F/Gas 5) and bake for 5–10 minutes longer, or until the pastries are puffed and golden–brown. Remove to a rack and let cool completely.

5   Split the profiteroles horizontally in half. Fill each with a scoop of vanilla ice cream. Set the tops in place, arrange on dessert plates, and drizzle the sauce over. Serve at once.

INGREDIENTS

115g (4oz) unsalted butter, cut into 8 pieces

240ml (8fl oz) water

1tsp sugar

½tsp salt

115g (4oz) plain flour

4 large eggs

1 litre (2 pints) Tahitian Double Vanilla (page 12), or your favourite premium brand

Chocolate Ganache (page 184) or Raspberry Sauce (page 66) or both

Serves 8

Frozen Coeur à la Crème with Balsamic Strawberries

Coeur à la crème is a French dessert, made of fresh mild cheese smothered in berries, traditionally served on Valentine's Day. Here a cream cheese ice cream does the trick, drenched with balsamic-marinated strawberries.

1 In a large bowl, combine the cream cheese, milk, lemon juice, sugar, vanilla extract, and salt. Beat until smooth. Add the double cream, mixing just until well-blended. Cover with cling film and refrigerate for 2 hours, or until cold.

2 Pour into the canister of an ice cream maker and freeze according to the manufacturer's directions.

3 Meanwhile, line a 17½–20cm (7–8in) heart-shaped mould with cling film, letting the ends fall over the sides of the mould. (Alternatively, line a 20cm or 8in round cake tin, or any other 1-litre mould.)

4 Scrape the cream cheese ice cream into the prepared mould, smoothing the top into an even layer. Wrap well and freeze for at least 2 hours, or until firm.

5 Unmould the ice cream heart onto a cold platter. Peel off the cling film. Let soften in the refrigerator for about 10 minutes before serving, with the balsamic berries on the side.

Balsamic Strawberries

In a large bowl, combine the strawberries, sugar, and vinegar. Toss gently to coat. Cover and let macerate at room temperature for 30 minutes to 1 hour. If made in advance, refrigerate for up to 8 hours.

INGREDIENTS

225g (8oz) cream cheese, softened

240ml (8fl oz) milk

1tbsp fresh lemon juice

175g (6oz) sugar

1tsp vanilla extract

Pinch of salt

120ml (4fl oz) double cream

Balsamic Strawberries (recipe follows)

Makes about 1 litre (2 pints)

Balsamic Strawberries

450g (1lb) strawberries, hulled and sliced

3–4tbsp sugar, depending upon the sweetness of the berries

1½tsp balsamic vinegar

Serves 4–6

Cassata

Cassata gelata is Sicilian in origin, and its flavours are based upon the traditional Easter treat comprised of sponge cake, ricotta cheese, and lots of candied fruits and nuts. Begin this frozen version 2 days before you plan to serve it.

1 In a small jar with a tight-fitting lid, combine the glacé fruits and rum. Cover and let stand at room temperature, stirring occasionally, for at least 2 hours or as long as 24 hours.

2 Trim the crusts and cut the cake lengthways into slices 1cm (⅜in) thick. Line a 900g (2lb) loaf tin with cling film, pressing it well into the corners and letting the ends drape over the sides by at least 7½cm (3in). Line the bottom and sides with cake slices.

3 Let the pistachio gelato stand at room temperature for 10–15 minutes to soften slightly. Spread it evenly over the bottom of the prepared pan, pressing gently to remove any air pockets. Cover the pan and freeze for about 2 hours, or until the gelato is firm.

4 Turn the vanilla gelato into a large bowl and let stand at room temperature for 10–15 minutes. Drain the fruits and add them to the gelato along with the chocolate chips. Fold and stir to incorporate them as evenly as possible. Pack into the loaf tin, cover again, and freeze for at least 2 hours.

5 Finally, soften the chocolate gelato by letting it stand at room temperature for 10–15 minutes. Spread it over the previous layers. Cover with any remaining slices of Madeira cake. Cover and freeze for at least 1 hour and up to 2 days. To serve, invert the cassata to unmould onto a platter. Carefully peel off the cling film. Let the loaf stand in the refrigerator for 5–10 minutes. Cut into thick slices and serve on chilled dessert plates with a drizzle of chocolate sauce over the top. If desired, garnish with orange peel and glacé fruits.

INGREDIENTS

4tbsp mixed glacé fruits

3tbsp dark rum or brandy

2 all-butter Madeira cakes, 305g (10¾oz) each

500ml (16fl oz) Pistachio Gelato (page 13), or your favourite premium brand ice cream or gelato

500ml (16fl oz) vanilla gelato or ice cream

4tbsp mini chocolate chips

500ml (16fl oz) chocolate gelato or ice cream

Easy Chocolate Sauce (page 184)

Sliced orange peel and glacé fruits, to garnish (optional)

Serves 8

Tartufo

These chocolate-coated ice cream treats are named for the black truffles they resemble. While they are often coated in a chocolate shell, at home it's easier to roll them in grated chocolate or drinking chocolate powder.

1 In a small jar, combine the cherries and brandy. Cover and let stand at room temperature, shaking occasionally, for at least 2 hours or as long as 24 hours. Line eight 8cm (3in) ramekins with squares of cling film. (Later you will need this excess to completely enclose the filling.)

2 Soften the chocolate ice cream at room temperature for 10–15 minutes. Spread it over the bottom and about two-thirds up the sides of the lined cups, leaving a deep well in the centre. Reserve about one-third of the ice cream to cover the tops of the cups later; return to the freezer until needed. Freeze the cups, covered, until the ice cream is firm to the touch, at least 1 hour.

3 Soften the hazelnut ice cream at room temperature for 10–15 minutes. Drain the cherries, reserving the brandy for another use. Fill the cavity in each cup with the hazelnut ice cream, then press a cherry into the centre of each. Freeze, covered, until firm to the touch, about 30 minutes.

4 Soften the remaining chocolate ice cream at room temperature for 5–10 minutes. Pack onto the tops of the moulds to cover completely. Cover and freeze until firm, at least 1 hour.

5 Use the ends of the cling film to lift the ice cream from the cup. Form the plastic-covered ice cream into balls. Twist the ends of the film to seal. Freeze until firm, at least 4 hours. To serve, unwrap the tartufo and roll in the grated chocolate to coat.

INGREDIENTS

8 maraschino cherries, stems removed, well-drained

4tbsp brandy or dark rum

500ml (16fl oz) Chocolate Custard Ice Cream (page 30), or your favourite premium brand ice cream or gelato

500ml (16fl oz) hazelnut ice cream or gelato, or any other flavour, such as coffee, cherry, or berry

60g (2oz) finely grated plain dark chocolate or 4tbsp drinking chocolate powder

Serves 8

Hidden Treasure
Ice Cream Cupcakes

Kids of all ages love the combination of cake and ice cream, and here the concept is made even more appealing with individual servings formed into ice cream cupcakes. The easy, egg-free batter bakes into a moist crumb, and the dessert can be made a week in advance and frozen.

1 Preheat the oven to 180°C (350°F/Gas 4). Line a 12-cup muffin tin with paper liners and set aside. In a large bowl, combine the flour, sugar, cocoa powder, bicarbonate of soda, and salt. Whisk to blend.

2 In another bowl, combine the water, oil, vinegar, and vanilla extract. Add to the dry ingredients, beating with an electric mixer until smooth.

3 Pour the batter into the muffin tins, filling each cup until approximately two-thirds full. Tap the pan on the counter to remove any air bubbles.

4 Bake for 25 minutes, or until a tester inserted in the centre of a cupcake comes out with moist crumbs clinging to it. Let the cupcakes cool in the pan for 5 minutes, then transfer them in their paper liners to a wire rack to cool completely.

5 With a serrated knife, cut the top third off of each cupcake and set aside. Using a melon baller or a serrated grapefruit knife, cut out the centre of the cupcake bottoms, leaving a 1cm (½in) shell all around and at the bottom. Place a small scoop of ice cream in the cupcake shell and replace the top; don't worry if some of the ice cream shows. If made in advance, wrap individually and freeze.

6 If serving with fudge sauce, peel off and discard the paper liners. Pour 2tbsp of fudge sauce on each dessert plate. Place the cupcake on top and serve with a spoon.

INGREDIENTS

175g (6oz) plain flour

225g (8oz) sugar

45g (1½oz) unsweetened cocoa powder

1tsp bicarbonate of soda

½tsp salt

240ml (8fl oz) cold water

75ml (2½fl oz) vegetable oil

1tbsp distilled white vinegar

1½tsp vanilla extract

500ml (16fl oz) White Chocolate Ice Cream (page 26), or your favourite home-made or store-bought flavour

Haute Fudge Sauce (optional; page 116)

Makes 12

COOL TIPS FOR SUCCESS

Serving frozen desserts on chilled plates will slow the melting process.

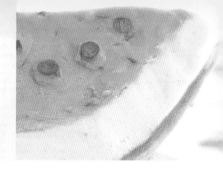

Watermelon Bombe

Here is a dessert that will bring a smile to everybody's face. What looks like a thick slice of watermelon is really an ice cream and sorbet surprise studded with chocolate chips.

1 Lightly spray the inside of a 1.4 litre (2½ pint) melon-shaped mould (about 23cm or 9in long) with nonstick cooking spray; freeze for at least 30 minutes. (Alternatively, line the inside of a 1.4 litre or 2½ pint freezer-safe bowl with 2 criss-crossed sheets of cling film, letting the plastic hang over the sides.) Refrigerate until needed.

2 Using a rubber spatula or a large spoon, spread the vanilla ice cream in the bottom and up the sides of the chilled mould, creating a cavity in the centre for the sorbet. Cover with cling film, pressing against the ice cream to seal tightly and press out any air pockets. Freeze for 4 hours, or until very firm.

3 Fold the chocolate chips into the softened sorbet. Pack the studded sorbet over the vanilla ice cream, pressing down to remove any air pockets. Cover again with cling film and freeze for 2 hours, or until firm.

4 Dip the mould into very hot water for 6 seconds to loosen. Remove the cling film and invert onto a chilled serving platter. Freeze until the ice cream is firm to the touch, about 15 minutes.

5 Use a few drops of undiluted food colouring to paint the outside of the moulded ice cream with a pastry brush. Do not try for uniform colour; variegated stripes are more realistic. Freeze for 15 minutes, or until the ice cream is firm to the touch. Cover tightly with cling film and freeze until very hard, at least 2 hours, or up to 3 days. Cut into thick slices with a long, sharp knife dipped in hot water and wiped dry. Serve at once on chilled dessert plates.

INGREDIENTS

750ml (1½ pints) Tahitian Double Vanilla Ice Cream (page 12), or your favourite vanilla ice cream, softened slightly

3tbsp mini chocolate chips

750ml (1½ pints) Watermelon-Raspberry Sorbet (page 96) or other pink or red sorbet, softened slightly

Green food colouring

Serves 6–8

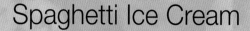

Spaghetti Ice Cream

In Italy, this is actually an adult dessert, but how much nicer for children: an ice-cold plate of frozen "spaghetti," complete with red sauce and cheese—even meatballs and garlic bread, if you like. To get the right effect, you'll need an old-fashioned potato ricer or spaetzle maker.

1 Place the potato ricer and a large platter in the freezer to chill for 15 minutes. In a small bowl, whisk the jam with a fork until it is soft and fluid.

2 Using a large serrated knife, cut crossways through the ice cream carton to divide the ice cream in half. Peel away the carton and pack the cold ice cream into the potato ricer. Use firm, steady pressure to push the ice cream slowly through the ricer, moving your hands in a circular motion to mimic the look of a plate of spaghetti. Repeat with the remaining ice cream.

3 Working quickly, drizzle with the jam. You can use the large holes on a box grater to grate white chocolate over the top to resemble Parmesan cheese. Return the platter to the freezer for 15 minutes, or until firm to the touch. Serve at once, or cover with cling film and freeze for up to 2 days. Let stand for 5–10 minutes in the refrigerator to soften slightly. Garnish with the "meatballs" and "garlic bread" just before serving.

INGREDIENTS

140g (5oz) strawberry jam or thick strawberry sauce

500ml (16fl oz) vanilla dairy ice cream, softened slightly but still firm enough to hold its shape

60g (2oz) white chocolate, at room temperature (optional)

Optional garnishes:

For meatballs, use small chocolate truffles, rolled in cocoa powder or finely chopped nuts.

For garlic bread, toast slices of Madeira cake and trim to resemble garlic bread. Top with a few tbsp of apricot jam mixed with 1tsp chopped fresh mint to simulate garlic butter.

Serves 2

Frozen Bonbons

Sometimes after a big meal, you want just a bite of something sweet. Here's a portion-controlled dessert that's perfect with after-dinner coffee or as a bite-sized snack in the late afternoon: miniature ice cream bonbons, coated with dark chocolate and frozen solid.

INGREDIENTS

500ml (16fl oz) of your favourite flavour ice cream, gelato, or frozen yoghurt

200g (7oz) plain dark chocolate

2tbsp sweet almond oil or melted unsalted butter

Pinch of salt

Makes about 2 dozen

1 Stack 2 baking sheets lined with baking parchment paper and place in the freezer until cold, about 15 minutes. Using a small (2½cm or 1in) ice cream scoop, a large melon baller, or a tablespoon, scoop out small balls of ice cream about 2½cm (1in) in diameter and set them on one of the sheets. Working quickly, insert a toothpick into the centre of each ice cream ball. Freeze for 3 hours, or until hard.

2 Place a small heatproof bowl over a pan of barely simmering water. Add the chocolate and cook over a very low heat, stirring, until melted and smooth. Remove from the heat, add the almond oil or butter and the salt, and stir until smooth.

3 Remove the ice cream balls from the freezer. Working quickly, one at a time, lift an ice cream ball by the toothpick and hold it over the bowl of melted chocolate. Ladle the melted chocolate over the ice cream ball, turning the ball to coat it completely, and letting the excess chocolate run back into the bowl. Place each finished ball on the second sheet in the freezer. Repeat with the remaining ice cream balls. Freeze for 4 hours, or until very firm. Remove the toothpicks. Serve at once, or cover with cling film and transfer to a freezer-safe container to store for up to 1 week.

Fruited Marsala Chestnut Bombes

While the flavour used to be associated with a lot of labour, these days, fully-cooked and peeled chestnuts are available in cans and vacuum-sealed packages in many supermarkets and delicatessens. *Crème de marrons* is sweetened chestnut purée, usually packaged in small cans. It comes plain or flavoured with vanilla. Either is fine for this recipe.

1 In a small bowl, combine the chopped chestnuts, currants, orange peel, glacé cherries, and Marsala wine. Cover and let stand at room temperature overnight. Drain the fruits, reserving the liquid.

2 Line four 8cm (3in) ramekins or moulds with enough cling film to drape generously over the sides.

3 Turn the ice cream into a large bowl and let stand at room temperature for about 10 minutes to soften slightly. Drop spoonfuls of the chopped chestnuts and fruits and 115g (4oz) of the chestnut purée over the ice cream. Using a stiff plastic spatula or a blunt knife, gently cut and fold to marble the ingredients into the ice cream. Don't worry if some larger pockets remain.

4 Pack the marbled ice cream into the lined moulds and cover each with cling film. Freeze until firm, at least 6 hours or overnight.

5 To make the sauce, mix together the remaining 60g (2oz) chestnut purée with the reserved Marsala wine. Remove each ice cream from its mould and invert onto a dessert plate; peel off the cling film. Drizzle about 2tbsp of the sauce over each dessert and top with whipped cream.

INGREDIENTS

115g (4oz) finely chopped, peeled, cooked chestnuts

1tbsp currants or raisins

1tbsp chopped candied orange peel

1tbsp chopped glacé red cherries

75ml (2½oz) sweet Marsala wine

500ml (16fl oz) Tahitian Double Vanilla Ice Cream (page 12), or your favourite premium brand

175g (6oz) chestnut purée (crème de marrons)

Whipped cream, for garnish

Serves 4

Warm Chocolate-Espresso Tart with Espresso Gelato

This decidedly adult combo contrasts a warm, intensely chocolate tart with a scoop of cold espresso-flavoured ice cream on the side. If you are lucky enough to have any of the tart left over the next day, it is also good served at room temperature or cold.

1 Preheat the oven to 190°C (375°F/Gas 5). In a medium saucepan, combine the cream, milk, espresso powder, and salt. Cook over a medium heat, stirring frequently, just until bubbles appear around the edges of the pan. Remove from the heat.

2 Add the chocolate to the hot espresso cream and stir until melted and smooth. Set aside and let cool to lukewarm, about 20 minutes. Whisk in the egg until thoroughly blended.

3 Place the prepared pastry shell on a baking sheet. Pour the chocolate filling into the shell. Bake for 12–15 minutes, or until the filling is almost firm but still trembling in the centre. Transfer to a wire rack and let cool for about 30 minutes.

4 To serve, remove the fluted sides of the tart pan. Cut the warm tart into wedges and transfer to individual dessert plates. Serve with a large scoop of Espresso Bean Gelato on the side. Dust with cocoa powder and serve at once.

INGREDIENTS

180ml (6fl oz) double cream

75ml (2½fl oz) milk

2tsp instant espresso powder

Pinch of salt

200g (7oz) plain dark chocolate, finely chopped

1 egg, lightly beaten

Shortcrust Pastry Shell, baked and cooled (page 186)

1 litre (2 pints) Espresso Bean Gelato (page 37), or store-bought coffee ice cream

Unsweetened cocoa powder, for dusting

Serves 8–10

Very Berry American Chocolate Shortcakes

How can you improve upon a traditional strawberry shortcake? Add ice cream and chocolate, of course!

1 In a large bowl, combine the berries, sugar, and lemon juice. Stir to mix, coarsely mashing about ¼ of the berries with a fork. Let stand for 15 minutes to dissolve the sugar.

2 To assemble, use a serrated knife to carefully split each scone in half horizontally. Place the bottom halves cut-sides up on 4 dessert plates. Top each with a large spoonful of berries and their juice and a scoop of ice cream. Cover with the scone tops. Dollop whipped cream over the shortcakes and top with the remaining berries. Garnish with Chocolate Curls and serve at once.

Chocolate-Buttermilk Scones

1 Preheat the oven to 220°C (425°F/Gas 7). In a food processor, combine the flour, cocoa powder, sugar, baking powder, bicarbonate of soda, and salt. Process briefly to blend. Add the butter and pulse until the dough resembles coarse crumbs. With the machine on, slowly pour in the buttermilk. Add the chocolate chips and pulse 2 or 3 times.

2 Scrape the dough onto a lightly floured work surface. Knead 2 or 3 times until smooth. Roll or pat the dough into an even 2½cm (1in) thickness. Using a 7½cm (3in) cookie cutter dipped in flour, cut out 4 scones. If needed, gather together the dough trimmings, pat them out again, and cut out more scones.

3 Arrange the scones 5cm (2in) apart on a parchment-lined baking sheet. Use a pastry brush to remove excess flour from the tops of the scones. Bake for 12–14 minutes, or until the tops spring back when touched lightly. Transfer to a wire rack to cool.

INGREDIENTS

450g (1lb) fresh berries (any combination of sliced strawberries or whole blueberries, raspberries, or blackberries)

1½tbsp sugar

1tsp fresh lemon juice

500ml (16fl oz) Almost-Instant Strawberry Ice Cream (page 20) or store-bought berry or vanilla ice cream

4 Chocolate-Buttermilk Scones (recipe follows)

Whipped cream, for garnish

Chocolate Curls (page 187)

Serves 4

Chocolate-Buttermilk Scones

115g (4oz) plain flour

4tbsp unsweetened cocoa powder

4tbsp sugar

1tsp baking powder

½tsp bicarbonate of soda

¼tsp salt

60g (2oz) cold unsalted butter, cut into 8 pieces

6tbsp buttermilk or 6tbsp milk mized with 1tsp lemon juice or vinegar

60g (2oz) chocolate chips

Makes 4 scones

Chocolate Ice Cream Sandwiches

These easy rolled chocolate cookies are the perfect texture for ice cream sandwiches: tender and not overly brittle.

1 In a medium bowl, combine the flour, cocoa powder, and salt. Whisk gently to blend the dry ingredients.

2 In a large bowl with an electric mixer, whisk the butter for 1 minute. Gradually whisk in the sugar until light and fluffy. Add the egg and vanilla and mix well. Gradually mix in the dry ingredients until well-blended. Cover and refrigerate for 2 hours, or until firm.

3 Preheat the oven to 180°C (350°F/Gas 4). On a lightly floured surface, roll out the cookie dough to a thickness of about 1cm (⅜in). You don't want these too thin. Cut out cookies with a 6cm (2½in) round cutter and carefully transfer them to 1 or 2 baking parchment-lined or lightly greased cookie sheets, spacing the cookies at least 2½cm (1in) apart. Gather any scraps into a ball and roll out to make more cookies.

4 Bake for 10–12 minutes, or until the bottoms are set. The tops will still be slightly soft; do not overbake. Transfer the cookies to a wire rack and let cool completely.

5 Arrange 12 cookies flat-side up on a baking sheet. Using a 5cm (2in) ice cream scoop or a large spoon, place about 60ml (2fl oz) of ice cream on each cookie. Cover with the remaining cookies, pressing down gently to form a sandwich. Smooth the edges, if desired. Working quickly, roll the sandwiches in the chocolate vermicelli or chopped nuts to coat the edges. Freeze uncovered until firm to the touch, about 30 minutes.

6 Wrap the sandwiches individually in squares of parchment or cling film. Place in an airtight container and freeze for at least 2 hours.

INGREDIENTS

175g (6oz) plain flour

85g (3oz) unsweetened cocoa powder

⅛tsp salt

175g (6oz) unsalted butter, at room temperature

225g (8oz) sugar

1 egg

½tsp vanilla extract

700ml (1½ pints) Tahitian Double Vanilla Ice Cream (page 12), or your favourite premium brand

½ cup chocolate vermicelli or finely chopped roasted peanuts or other nuts

Makes about 2 dozen (6cm or 2½in) cookies, to make 12 sandwiches

Chocolate Chip Birthday "Pizza" with Ice Cream Balls

Three of kids' favourite foods all bound up in one: a chocolate chip ice cream pizza. If you prefer to serve the pizza directly from the pan, omit the baking parchment and simply grease and flour the baking sheet instead.

1 Preheat the oven to 190°C (375°F/Gas 5). Line a pizza pan or large cookie sheet with a 35cm (14in) round of baking parchment paper. In a medium bowl, combine the flour, bicarbonate of soda, and salt; set the dry ingredients aside.

2 In a large bowl, combine the butter, brown sugar, granulated sugar, and vanilla extract. Whisk with an electric mixer until light and creamy. Whisk in the egg until well-blended. With the mixer on low, gradually add the dry ingredients. Mix in the chocolate chips by hand until just blended. Scrape the dough onto the baking parchment and pat into an even layer 30cm (12in) in diameter.

3 Bake for 20–25 minutes, or until the centre is set; the edges need not be browned. Transfer the pan to a wire rack and let cool completely. Carefully slide the cookie "pizza" onto a large serving platter, using the ends of the baking parchment to help pull; otherwise, leave on the pan. Cover tightly with cling film and freeze until cold, at least 30 minutes or up to 4 days.

4 Spread an even layer of softened vanilla ice cream over the top. Cover and freeze for 30 minutes. Then, working quickly and using a small 4cm (1½in) ice cream scoop, dollop round balls of chocolate and strawberry ice cream all over the cookie crust. Decorate with hundreds & thousands and Chocolate Curls and freeze uncovered until firm; then wrap in cling film.

5 About 30 minutes before serving, unwrap the "pizza" and let soften in the refrigerator for 15–20 minutes before cutting.

INGREDIENTS

250g (9oz) plain flour

1tsp bicarbonate of soda

½tsp salt

225g (8oz) unsalted butter, at room temperature

225g (8oz) dark brown sugar

4tbsp granulated sugar

2tsp vanilla extract

1 egg

350g (12oz) plain chocolate chips

500ml (16fl oz) Tahitian Double Vanilla Ice Cream (page 12), or your favourite premium brand, softened slightly

500ml (16fl oz) Chocolate Custard Ice Cream (page 30), or your favourite premium brand

500ml (16fl oz) Almost-Instant Strawberry Ice Cream (page 20), or your favourite premium brand

Hundreds & thousands and Chocolate Curls (page 187), for garnish

Serves 10–12

Frozen Chocolate Dessert Lollies

Boiled custard is unbelievably easy. This one is eggless, so there is no worry of curdling—and it's ready for the freezer in 15 minutes or less.

1 In a medium saucepan, combine the sugar, cocoa, cornflour, and salt. Whisk gently to blend. Place over a medium heat and gradually whisk in the milk. Bring to the boil, whisking until thickened and smooth, 5–7 minutes. Remove from the heat and add the chocolate chips; stir until melted and smooth. Stir in the vanilla extract and set aside for 5 minutes to cool slightly.

2 Divide the custard among eight (120–150ml or 4–5fl oz) ice lolly moulds or paper cups and freeze for 1 hour, or until partially frozen. Insert a wooden ice lolly stick or sturdy plastic spoon into the centre of each cup. Freeze for 4 hours, or until very firm.

3 Unmould; or, if using cups, tear off the paper. Serve at once, or cover with cling film and store in the freezer for up to 3 days.

INGREDIENTS

140g (5oz) sugar

4tbsp unsweetened cocoa powder

4tbsp cornflour

¼tsp salt

750ml (1¼ pints) milk

85g (3oz) plain chocolate chips

½tsp vanilla extract

Makes 8 lollies

Fruit Smoothie Ice Lollies

Keep a batch of these healthy snacks in the freezer, and kids can help themselves anytime they like. Appropriate wooden ice lolly sticks are sold in craft stores and in some supermarkets.

1 In a blender, combine the fruit, milk, yoghurt, and honey. Process for 30 seconds, or until thick and smooth.

2 Pour into eight (120–150ml or 4–5fl oz) ice lolly moulds or paper cups and freeze for 1 hour or until partially frozen. Insert a wooden ice lolly stick or sturdy plastic spoon into the centre of each cup. Freeze for 3 hours, or until very firm.

3 Unmould or, if using cups, tear off the paper. Serve at once, or cover with cling film and store in the freezer for up to 3 days.

INGREDIENTS

225g (8oz) assorted fruits, such as bananas, strawberries, raspberries, and peaches

360ml (12fl oz) milk

225g (8oz) plain yoghurt

5tbsp honey or maple syrup

Makes about 8 lollies

"we dare not trust our wit
for making our house pleasant to
our friends, so we buy
ice cream."

–writer Ralph Waldo Emerson

almost–instant frozen desserts

Chocolate Cookie Ice Cream Cake

Here's an almost-instant cake the kids will love. As long as the cake is tightly wrapped, it can be made weeks in advance and frozen, so it's all ready to be pulled out whenever you need a dessert everyone will love.

1 Preheat the oven to 190°C (375°F/Gas 5). Spread out the almonds on a small baking sheet and toast them in the oven until lightly browned, 10–12 minutes. Transfer to a plate and let cool.

2 Break up the cookies roughly into quarters. In 2 batches, combine the toasted almonds and chocolate cookies in a food processor and pulse to chop very coarsely. Transfer to a bowl and mix in the chocolate chips.

3 Line the bottom of a round 20–23cm (8–9in) greaseproof springform pan with waxed paper, baking parchment, or foil. Open the ice cream and use a large knife to cut into 2–2½cm (¾–1in) slices. As you cut each slice, fit it flat against the bottom of the pan. When most of the bottom is covered, smooth with a stiff plastic spatula or large metal spoon to fill in any gaps. Sprinkle one-third of the chocolate-almond crumbs over the ice cream to make an even layer. Cover with another layer of ice cream and another layer of the chocolate-almond crumbs. Repeat the layers until all the ice cream and crumbs have been used. Double wrap in cling film and freeze.

4 A couple of hours before serving, remove the cake from the freezer and unwrap. Using a blunt knife dipped in hot water and wiped dry, cut around the sides of the pan to separate the ice cream from the pan. Remove the sides of the pan. Smooth the sides of the cake with a rubber spatula and place in the freezer for 5–10 minutes to firm up; then re-wrap the cake and return to the freezer until serving time.

INGREDIENTS

60g (2oz) shelled almonds

125g (4½oz) chocolate cookies

125g (4½oz) mini chocolate chips

2 litre carton of vanilla dairy ice cream

Serves 8–10

Frozen Cannoli

These are instant in the sense that you don't have to make anything, but the assembled cannoli must be filled in advance so that they have time to set fully in the freezer. Choose a sauce that complements the flavour of ice cream you've chosen, and if using chocolate or toffee sauce, heat gently before serving. Cannoli tubes can be purchased from some Italian delis or ordered online.

1 Let the ice cream stand at room temperature for 10–15 minutes to soften slightly. Fit a large pastry bag with a large plain tip or use a large heavy-duty ziplock plastic bag and cut off one of the bottom corners. Fill with the ice cream.

2 Working quickly with one cannoli at a time, insert the tip of the pastry bag into the cannoli tube and fill with ice cream. Place the filled cannoli on a baking sheet and place in the freezer for at least 2 hours or overnight.

3 Remove the ice cream–filled cannoli from the freezer 10–15 minutes before serving. Meanwhile, warm the sauce over a low heat, if needed. Place each cannoli on a dessert plate and drizzle with the sauce of your choice. Sprinkle the cannoli with nuts and serve at once.

INGREDIENTS

750ml (1½ pints) ice cream, your choice of flavour

12 cannoli tubes

240ml (8fl oz) Easy Chocolate Sauce (page 187), Toffee Sauce (page 185), or Raspberry Sauce (page 66)

Chopped toasted almonds, walnuts, or pistachios, for garnish

Serves 6

Rainbow Ice Cream
and Sorbet Torte

This super-easy, sophisticated-looking frozen torte draws its inspiration from the classic children's ice lolly treat, layering fruit sorbet and ice cream. Top with a few fresh raspberries and a sprig of mint, or a drizzle of Raspberry Sauce (page 66), if you like.

1 Let the orange sherbet soften enough so you can scoop it out easily. Pack into the bottom of a 23cm (9in) springform pan. Cover with cling film and freeze for 30–60 minutes, or until the sherbet hardens.

2 Let half of the ice cream soften slightly. Pack that over the sherbet. Cover and return to the freezer until set.

3 Let the Watermelon-Raspberry Sorbet soften slightly. Pack that over the ice cream.

4 Soften the other half of the ice cream and pack that over the Watermelon-Raspberry Sorbet. Cover and freeze for at least 2 hours, or overnight.

5 To serve, dip a blunt knife in a glass of hot water, quickly wipe it dry, and run the warm knife around the edge of the springform pan. Remove the sides. Supporting the torte on the metal bottom, rotate the dessert while pressing the chopped pistachios into the side to coat completely.

6 Set the torte on a warm, damp towel for about 10 seconds to loosen the bottom. Invert onto a large round platter and carefully remove the metal bottom of the pan. If necessary, smooth the top of the torte with a warm spatula. Cut into wedges to serve.

INGREDIENTS

500ml (16fl oz) Orange Sherbet (page 49), or store-bought orange sorbet

1 litre (2 pints) vanilla dairy ice cream

500ml (16fl oz) Watermelon-Raspberry Sorbet (page 96), or store-bought raspberry sorbet

85g (3oz) chopped pistachio nuts

Serves 10–12

Mile-High Lemon Chiffon Ice Cream Pie

Lofty enough to make an impression, this airy ice cream pie also has a pronounced lemon flavour. It's one dessert you can make well ahead of time, because the texture actually improves after several days in the freezer. Lemon curd is usually found in the jams and marmalades section of the supermarket.

1 In a large bowl, whisk the egg whites and salt until the whites stand in soft, foamy peaks. Continue to whisk as you gradually add the sugar in a thin, steady stream. Whisk until the whites stand in stiff, firm peaks.

2 In a small bowl, whisk together the lemon curd, lemon rind, and lemon juice. Using a large rubber spatula, carefully fold the lemon curd mixture into the whisked egg whites until evenly incorporated without deflating the whites.

3 Place the ice cream in a large bowl and mash with a rubber spatula to make it malleable, but not melted. Working quickly, scoop the egg whites over the ice cream and fold until the mixture is almost blended; it's okay if there are a few white streaks. Pile into the prepared crust, mounding it in the centre, and immediately place the pie in the freezer. Freeze for at least 6 hours.

4 If you are not serving the pie the same day, carefully cover it with cling film and freeze for up to 4 days. To serve, let the pie sit in the refrigerator for 15 minutes before slicing into wedges with a long, sharp knife dipped in hot water and wiped dry.

INGREDIENTS

4 egg whites

Pinch of salt

5tbsp sugar

250g (9oz) lemon curd

1tbsp grated lemon rind

2tbsp fresh lemon juice

1½ litres (3 pints) vanilla ice cream, softened slightly

Ginger Nut Crumb Crust (page 186), or a 23cm (9in) sweet pastry crust, chilled

Serves 6–8

COOL TIPS FOR SUCCESS

Frozen pies and other desserts benefit from softening in the refrigerator for 10 minutes (or as the recipe directs) before serving. The ice cream should be firm, but just manageable enough to scoop or slice. Remember that once cut, individual servings of home-made ice cream will soften quickly.

Island Frozen Yoghurt Pie with Banana-Rum Sauce

Frozen yoghurt nestled in a crunchy cereal crust sounds innocent enough . . . until it is bathed in a decadent Toffee Banana-Rum Sauce.

1 Preheat the oven to 190°C (375°F/Gas 5). Lightly coat a 23cm (9in) pie tin with cooking spray. In a large bowl, crush the cereal with your fingers until it is broken into crumbs.

2 Melt the butter in a small saucepan over a low heat, or in the microwave in a microwave-safe container. Add the sugar, stirring until it is dissolved. Add to the crushed cereal, stirring to coat. Press the mixture onto the bottom and up the sides of the prepared pie tin. Bake 10–12 minutes or until the crust is set and lightly browned at the edges. Transfer to a wire rack to cool completely.

3 Soften the frozen yoghurt by letting it stand at room temperature for 10 minutes. Pack the yoghurt into the cool shell, pressing down lightly to remove any air pockets. Cover the surface of the yoghurt with cling film and freeze until firm, at least 4 hours or overnight.

4 To serve, let the pie soften for 15 minutes in the refrigerator before cutting into wedges with a long, sharp knife dipped in hot water and wiped dry. Top each serving with a drizzle of Toffee Banana-Rum Sauce.

INGREDIENTS

5 Weetabix® biscuits

75g (2½oz) unsalted butter

2tbsp light or dark brown sugar

1 litre (2 pints) vanilla or dulce de leche frozen yoghurt

Toffee Banana-Rum Sauce (page 185)

Serves 8

Chocolate–Peanut Butter Pie

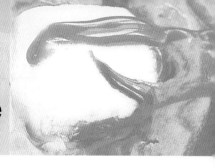

There are certain kinds of people who cannot get enough of chocolate and peanut butter. This frozen pie is dedicated to them, as well as to those who love them. It is a sweet dessert, so portion accordingly.

1 Prepare and bake the crust as directed. Let cool, then place in the freezer to chill thoroughly.

2 In a large bowl, combine the softened vanilla and chocolate ice cream, the peanuts, and the marshmallows. Using a large wooden spoon or stiff plastic spatula, stir and mash them together, working until the ice creams are marbled with prominent streaks of chocolate and vanilla. Drop heaping spoonfuls of both the peanut butter and chocolate sauce over the mixture. Working quickly, stir and mash them into the ice cream, blending only partially, so you also see streaks of peanut butter and chocolate in the ice cream.

3 Pile the mixture into the prepared crust, mounding it in the centre. Freeze for at least 6 hours before serving. If you are not serving the pie the same day, carefully cover it with cling film and freeze for up to 3 days.

4 To serve, let the pie stand in the refrigerator for 15 minutes before slicing into wedges with a long, sharp knife dipped in hot water and wiped dry.

INGREDIENTS

Chocolate Crumb Crust (page 187), or a 23cm (9in) prepared chocolate cookie crust

700ml (1½ pints) vanilla ice cream, softened slightly

700ml (1½ pints) chocolate ice cream, softened slightly

60g (2oz) coarsely chopped roasted peanuts (salted or unsalted)

60g (2oz) miniature marshmallows

250g (9oz) smooth peanut butter, chilled

150ml (5fl oz) chocolate or fudge sauce or topping (not chocolate syrup), home-made or store-bought, chilled

Serves 6–8

Frozen Mississippi Mud Pie

In Mississippi, people say their chocolate-crusted ice cream pie drenched in fudge sauce is made from "mud." Southwesterners refer to their version as "adobe." Whatever you call it, this sumptuous dessert is perfect for casual entertaining, because you can make it several days in advance and hold it in the freezer.

1 Prepare the Chocolate Crumb Crust as directed and chill thoroughly.

2 Pour about 120ml (4fl oz) of the Mocha Fudge Sauce into the crust. Spread it evenly and freeze for 30 minutes, or until firm.

3 Working quickly, use a rubber spatula to spread the vanilla ice cream over the fudge sauce, mounding it slightly in the centre. Cover with cling film and freeze for 1 hour, or until firm.

4 Spread the coffee ice cream in an even layer over the vanilla, again mounding it slightly in the centre. Sprinkle Chocolate Curls all over the top of the pie. Freeze for 1 hour. Carefully cover with cling film and freeze for at least 5 more hours or up to 4 days.

5 To serve, let the pie sit in the refrigerator for about 15 minutes to soften just slightly before slicing into wedges with a long, sharp knife dipped in hot water and wiped dry. Drizzle a couple of tbsp of Mocha Fudge Sauce on the side—not over—each slice.

INGREDIENTS

Chocolate Crumb Crust (page 187), or a 23cm (9in) prepared chocolate cookie crust

Mocha Fudge Sauce (page 184), or your favourite chocolate sauce

700ml (1½ pints) vanilla ice cream, softened slightly

700ml (1½ pints) coffee ice cream, softened slightly

Chocolate Curls (page 187) or 60g (2oz) plain dark chocolate, coarsely grated

Serves 6–8

Mocha Madness
Ice Cream Pie

One taste of this easy-to-make pie, and you'll understand why it is so popular. The chocolate cereal "crust" ends up tasting like an aerated chocolate bar. If you like, vary the ice cream flavour to suit your mood, or try using white chocolate or milk chocolate chips instead of plain chocolate.

1 Press a 30cm (12in) sheet of foil into the bottom and up the sides of a 23cm (9in) pie tin, letting the excess drape over the edge. Spray with cooking spray.

2 Place a large heatproof bowl over a pot of barely simmering water. Add the chocolate and butter and cook over a low heat, stirring, until melted and smooth. Add the cereal, stirring to coat well. Using the back of a spoon, form a shell by pressing the warm mixture into the bottom and up the sides of the foil in the prepared pie tin. Freeze for 30 minutes, or until the shell is very cold and firm. Use the edges of the foil to remove the crisped rice shell from the pan. Carefully peel off and discard the foil; return the shell to the tin.

3 Soften the ice cream by letting it stand at room temperature for 10 minutes. Pack the ice cream into the cold shell, pressing down lightly to remove any air pockets. Cover and freeze until the ice cream is very firm, at least 4 hours or up to 3 days.

4 To serve, let the pie soften for 15 minutes in the refrigerator. Spoon or pipe the whipped cream over the top of the pie. Garnish with chocolate-covered espresso beans and chocolate shavings. Cut into wedges with a long, sharp knife dipped in hot water and wiped dry. Serve warm, with Mocha Fudge Sauce on the side.

INGREDIENTS

85g (3oz) plain chocolate chips

30g (1oz) unsalted butter, cut into pieces

60g (2oz) crisped rice cereal (such as Kellogg's Rice Krispies®)

1 litre (2 pints) coffee ice cream

240ml (8fl oz) double cream, whipped

Chocolate-covered espresso beans and chocolate shavings, for garnish

Mocha Fudge Sauce (page 184)

Serves 8

Ice Cream Cupcakes

This combines everything kids love at a birthday party: hundreds & thousands, chocolate chip cookies, ice cream, individual portions, and no plates or utensils! These can be completely assembled and frozen weeks in advance if you use long-life whipping cream instead of fresh whipped cream. But if you wait and allow the children to squirt instant aerosol whipped cream onto their own cakes, they will surely deem your party the social event of the season.

1 Preheat the oven to 180°C (350°F/Gas 4). Line 2 standard 12-cup muffin tins with paper liners.

2 Cut the cookie dough into 24 squares. Place 1 piece of dough in each lined muffin cup.

3 Bake for 10–12 minutes, or until the cookies are barely set. They will firm up as they cool. Let cool completely in the tins.

4 Place 1 small scoop of ice cream on top of each cookie. Press down gently with the back of a spoon to remove any air pockets. If using long-life whipping cream, whisk into stiff peaks and spread over the ice cream. Cover the tins with cling film and freeze for at least 4 hours or as long as 1 week. Once the cupcakes are frozen, they can be removed from the metal tins and stored in an airtight container.

5 If using instant aerosol whipped cream, squirt it on just before serving. Garnish with the hundreds & thousands or vermicelli.

INGREDIENTS

500g (1lb 2oz) frozen or chilled chocolate chip cookie dough

2 litres (4 pints) of your child's favourite flavour ice cream

300ml (10fl oz) long-life whipping cream or 250g (9oz) instant aerosol whipped cream

Hundreds & thousands or chocolate vermicelli, for garnish

Makes 24 cupcakes

Phony Spumoni

Italian spumoni is gelato, often a couple of flavours, usually lightened with whipped cream and blended with crystallised fruit and nuts. This simplified version mixes vanilla ice cream with toasted almonds, pistachio nuts, maraschino cherries, candied orange peel, and dark chocolate to simulate the more sophisticated dessert.

1 Preheat the oven to 160°C (325°F/Gas 3). Line a 20cm (8in) round cake tin with cling film, leaving enough extra to extend over the rim of the tin.

2 Spread out the almond slices in a small baking pan and toast in the oven until lightly browned and fragrant, 5–7 minutes. Transfer to a plate and let cool. Coarsely chop 2tbsp of the almonds.

3 Let the ice cream stand at room temperature for 10–15 minutes so that it is just malleable. Quickly stir in the chopped toasted almonds, pistachio nuts, chocolate, chopped cherries with the reserved juice, and candied orange peel. Be sure to distribute the ingredients as evenly as possible.

4 Spread the spumoni into the plastic-lined cake tin and smooth the top with a spatula. Cover with cling film and freeze for at least 4 hours, until completely set.

5 To serve, unwrap the spumoni and invert to unmould onto a large serving plate. Carefully peel off the cling film from the top. If necessary, smooth the top of the ice cream with a spatula. Press the remaining toasted almonds around the sides of the spumoni. Cut into wedges and serve immediately.

INGREDIENTS

30g (1oz) flaked almonds

1½ litres (3 pints) vanilla ice cream

30g (1oz) coarsely chopped pistachio nuts

30g (1oz) finely chopped plain dark chocolate

60g (2oz) maraschino cherries, drained with 1tbsp juice reserved, coarsely chopped

3tbsp chopped candied orange peel

Serves 8–10

COOL TIPS FOR SUCCESS

When serving frozen desserts, dip the knife, spoon, or scoop in hot water and quickly blot dry with a towel between each serving.

Ice Cream and Sorbet Lollies

Use any combination of sorbet and ice cream here to make your own ice lollies.

1 Pack about 4tbsp of sorbet into eight (120–150ml or 4–5fl oz) ice lolly moulds or paper cups, pressing firmly to remove any air pockets. If there is any sorbet left over, divide it equally among the moulds, pressing down firmly. Freeze for 30 minutes, until partially frozen.

2 Pack about 4tbsp of the ice cream into the moulds, packing down gently to remove any air pockets. If there is any ice cream left over, divide it equally among the moulds, pressing down gently. Freeze for 30 minutes or until partially frozen.

3 Insert a wooden ice lolly stick or a sturdy plastic spoon into the centre of each cup. Freeze for 3 hours or until very firm. Unmould or, if using cups, tear off the paper. Serve at once, or cover with cling film and store in the freezer for up to 1 week.

INGREDIENTS

500ml (16fl oz) orange or raspberry sorbet
500ml (16fl oz) vanilla ice cream

Serves 8

"the only emperor is the emperor of ice cream."

–poet Wallace Stevens

ice cream sodas, milkshakes, & floats

"Manhattan" Float

Inspired by Boston chef Gabriel Frasca's brilliant creation, this grown-up float is the quintessential hybrid cocktail-dessert. Always remember that the better the quality of the bourbon whiskey you use, the better the finished drink will taste.

1 In a small jar with a tight-fitting lid, combine 2tbsp of the bourbon with the cherries. Cover and let sit at room temperature, shaking occasionally, for at least 2 hours or as long as 24 hours. Drain the cherries, reserving the bourbon.

2 In a large bowl, combine the ice cream with the remaining 90ml (3fl oz) bourbon and the cherry juice. Using a rubber spatula or a wooden spoon, stir until well-blended. Cover tightly with cling film and freeze until firm, at least 2 hours. Place 4 tall glasses in the freezer or refrigerator to chill.

3 In another large bowl, combine the cream, vermouth, icing sugar, and bitters. Whisk with an electric mixer until soft peaks form.

4 Put 2 scoops of ice cream in each chilled glass. Top with enough coke to reach within 1cm (½in) of the rim. Rub the cut edge of an orange peel strip over the rim of each glass and twist it over the drink to release the oils, then discard. Drizzle the reserved bourbon over each float. Top with a generous dollop of the flavoured whipped cream and a cherry. Serve at once.

INGREDIENTS

120ml (4fl oz) bourbon whiskey

4 maraschino cherries with stems

1 litre (2 pints) Tahitian Double Vanilla Ice Cream (page 12), or your favourite premium brand, slightly softened

1tbsp maraschino cherry juice (from the jar of cherries)

240ml (8fl oz) double cream, chilled

1½tbsp sweet vermouth

1½tbsp icing sugar

Dash of aromatic bitters, such as Angostura®

1 litre (1¾ pints) Coca Cola® cherry coke, chilled

4 strips of fresh orange peel

Serves 4

Sensational
Strawberry Shake

Strawberries provide a tart undertone to offset the richness of the ice cream.

In a blender or food processor, combine the ice cream, strawberries, and milk. Process until well-blended but still thick. Pour into tall, chilled glasses and serve at once.

INGREDIENTS

700ml (1½ pints) Almost-Instant Strawberry Ice Cream (page 20), Tahitian Double Vanilla Ice Cream (page 12), or store-bought strawberry or vanilla ice cream

280g (10oz) fresh strawberries, hulled

240ml (8fl oz) milk, chilled

Makes 2 large shakes

VARIATION

Very Berry Shake: Substitute a combination of 450g (1lb) fresh or frozen raspberries, blackberries, or blueberries for the strawberries.

Strawberry Sweetheart Soda

Some people just can't get enough of the color pink. Here it is in all its glory, in a delectable soda little girls of all ages will love.

1 Place 3tbsp of strawberry sauce in each glass. Stir 2tbsp single cream or milk into each. Add 1 small scoop of ice cream; stir and mash to dissolve partially.

2 Add about 75ml (2½fl oz) sparkling mineral water to each, letting the foam rise to the top. Scoop in the remaining ice cream and top off with the remaining mineral water. Top with whipped cream and a strawberry or maraschino cherry and serve at once.

INGREDIENTS

6tbsp Simple Strawberry Sauce (page 112), or store-bought strawberry syrup

4tbsp single cream or milk

700ml (1½ pints) Almost-Instant Strawberry Ice Cream (page 20), Tahitian Double Vanilla Ice Cream (page 12), or store-bought strawberry or vanilla ice cream

240ml (8fl oz) sparkling mineral water or soda water, chilled

Whipped cream, for garnish

2 fresh strawberries or maraschino cherries, for garnish

Makes 2 large sodas

Mango Sorbet Float

Manoeuvering a spoon in and out of a fragile champagne flute can be risky. Instead, serve this festive sparkling "float" in a wine glass that has a wider bowl.

Place 1 scoop of sorbet in each of 6 large chilled wine glasses. Pour about 120ml (4fl oz) of the Prosecco in each and serve at once.

INGREDIENTS

750ml (1½ pints) Mango-Pineapple Sorbet (page 88), or store-bought mango sorbet

1 bottle (750 ml) Prosecco or other dry but fruity sparkling wine

Serves 6

VARIATION

Mango-Raspberry Float: Put a small scoop of mango sorbet and a small scoop of raspberry sorbet into 6–8 tall glasses. Divide a bottle (750 ml) of Prosecco among the glasses. Garnish each with a few raspberries, if you have them.

Lemon Vodka Martini Shake

Get a head start on summer entertaining by stashing a batch or two of this refreshing cocktail in your freezer. Pour into freezer-safe martini glasses (not your best crystal) or plastic tumblers and—voila!—drinks are ready when the guests arrive. Because of the alcohol content, these remain seductively soft and slushy in the freezer. As summer goes on, you may wish to vary the flavour of sorbet and vodka— raspberry makes a strikingly beautiful (and delicious) shake.

In a blender or food processor, combine the sorbet, ice, vodka, and lemon juice. Process just until blended. Pour into glasses and serve at once, or cover each glass tightly with cling film and freeze for up to 1 week. To serve, garnish each with a lemon twist, if desired.

INGREDIENTS

500ml (16fl oz) Meyer Lemon Sorbet (page 84), or store-bought lemon sorbet

360ml (12fl oz) crushed ice

240ml (8fl oz) chilled lemon-flavoured or plain vodka, or more to taste

6tbsp fresh lemon juice

Lemon twists

Serves 6–8

Lime-in-the-Coconut Shake

One sip and you'll be transported to a warm beach, wiggling your toes in the sand and listening to the sounds of a steel drum band in the distance. At your fantasy island resort, this would probably be served in a coconut shell with a paper parasol and all the other fancy accoutrements, but back in the real world that seems like overkill for such an easily-made beverage. Don't try to cut corners by omitting the toasted coconut — it ties together all of the flavours.

1 Preheat the oven to 180°C (350°F/Gas 4). Spread out the coconut evenly in a small shallow pan. Toast in the oven, stirring frequently, for 7–10 minutes, or until lightly browned. Set aside to cool.

2 In a blender or food processor, combine the ice cream, coconut milk, and lime juice cordial. Process until well-blended but still thick.

3 Divide among 4 tall, chilled glasses. Top each with a dollop of whipped cream and 2tbsp of toasted coconut. Garnish with a slice of lime and serve at once.

INGREDIENTS

60g (2oz) desiccated coconut

700ml (1½ pints) Tahitian Double Vanilla Ice Cream (page 12) or store-bought vanilla ice cream or frozen yoghurt

1 can (400ml or 14fl oz) light or regular coconut milk, chilled and well-shaken

120ml (4fl oz) lime juice cordial

Whipped cream, for garnish

4 lime slices, for garnish

Makes 4 servings

California Date Shake

Ranchers in the southern California desert grow over 99 per cent of the dates sold in America. Due to the accessibility of this local crop, many restaurants and soda fountains in nearby towns tempt travelers with highway billboards advertising ice cold date shakes as relief for parched palates. The chewy bits of date scattered throughout the creamy shake make for an interesting textural contrast, as well as an exceptional burst of flavour.

In a blender or food processor, combine the dates and milk. Process until the dates are finely chopped. Add the ice cream and vanilla extract and process until well-blended but still thick. Pour into tall, chilled glasses and serve at once.

INGREDIENTS

200g (7oz) whole stoned dates

240ml (8fl oz) milk, chilled

700ml (1½ pints) Tahitian Double Vanilla Ice Cream (page 12), or store-bought vanilla ice cream

½tsp vanilla extract

Makes 2 large servings

VARIATION

Banana-Date Shake: In a blender or food processor, combine 1 ripe banana with 100g (3½oz) stoned dates. Process until the dates are finely chopped. Add the ice cream and milk and process until well-blended but still thick. Pour into tall, chilled glasses and serve at once.

Ice Cream
with Spiked Espresso

Long before espresso entered the British coffee vocabulary, savvy Italians made *affogato* by "drowning" gelato in hot espresso. For a seriously adult dessert, take this excellent idea one step further by adding a generous splash of your favorite liqueur. (And a puffy cloud of whipped cream never hurts, either.)

1 Divide the ice cream among 4 heatproof glasses, coffee cups, or bowls. (This can be done several hours in advance and kept covered in the freezer.)

2 Just before serving, pour 4tbsp hot espresso and 2tbsp of the liqueur over each portion of ice cream. Top with whipped cream and hazelnuts, if desired. Serve at once.

INGREDIENTS

500ml (16fl oz) vanilla or coffee gelato

240ml (8fl oz) hot, freshly brewed espresso or strong coffee (regular or decaf)

½ cup hazelnut liqueur, such as Frangelico®, coffee liqueur, dark rum, or brandy

Whipped cream and/or chopped toasted hazelnuts, for garnish

Serves 4

Macchiato Milkshake

Macchiato literally means dotted, which here translates to foamed milk on top of espresso, as well as an irresistibly elegant shake.

In a blender or food processor, combine the ice cream, milk, and espresso. Process until well-blended but still thick. Pour into tall, chilled glasses and serve at once.

INGREDIENTS

1 litre (2 pints) Coffee Ice Cream (page 32), or your favourite premium brand

180ml (6fl oz) milk

180ml (6fl oz) brewed espresso or strong coffee, chilled

Makes 2 large shakes

VARIATION

Macchiato-Kahlúa Milkshake: In a blender or food processor, combine the ice cream, milk, and espresso as directed above. Add 4tbsp Kahlúa or other coffee-flavoured liqueur. Process until well-blended but still thick. Pour into tall, chilled glasses and serve at once.

Black and White Ice Cream Soda

This all-time classic soda gets its name from the "black" chocolate syrup and the "white" vanilla ice cream. However you refer to it, it remains one of the greatest ice cream drinks ever invented.

1 Place 3tbsp of chocolate syrup in each glass. Stir in 2tbsp single cream. Add 1 small scoop of ice cream, stirring and mashing to blend.

2 Pour about 75ml (2½fl oz) sparkling water into each, letting foam rise to the top. Scoop in the remaining ice cream and top off with the remaining sparkling water. Top with whipped cream and a cherry and serve at once.

Chocolate Syrup

1 In a medium saucepan, combine the sugar, cocoa powder, and salt. Gradually whisk in the water until smooth.

2 Bring to the boil over a medium heat, stirring to dissolve the sugar. Cook for 3 minutes longer, stirring constantly. Remove from the heat and let cool. Stir in the vanilla extract. Serve at once, or refrigerate, covered, for up to 1 week.

INGREDIENTS

90ml (3fl oz) Chocolate Syrup (recipe follows) or your favourite brand

4tbsp single cream or milk

4 scoops of Tahitian Double Vanilla Ice Cream (page 12), or your favourite premium brand

240ml (8fl oz) sparkling mineral water or soda water, chilled

Whipped cream, for garnish

2 maraschino cherries, for garnish

Makes 2 large shakes

Chocolate Syrup

225g (8oz) sugar

60g (2oz) unsweetened cocoa powder

Pinch of salt

240ml (8fl oz) water

1tsp vanilla extract

Makes about 550ml (18fl oz)

Chocolate Mini-Malts
with Madeira Cake "Chips"

Sometimes it's fun to end a dinner party with a whimsical dessert, especially if it tastes as clever as it looks. Although most of us would never consider ordering a huge milkshake after dinner, a small juice glass containing just a few sips is a reasonable indulgence. And to round out the nostalgic feeling, a side order of "chips" is added to the plate. You could even give each guest a tablespoon or two of Simple Strawberry Sauce (page 170) as tomato "ketchup" for their chips.

1 Preheat the oven to 160°C (325°F/Gas 3). Slice off the rounded top of the cake, as well as the dark outer crust on the bottom and sides of the loaf. Cut the cake in half crossways; then cut each half horizontally into 3 slices about 1cm (½in) thick. Working with half of the cake at a time, stack the layers and cut into strips about 1cm (½in) wide and about 9cm (3½in) long to resemble chips.

2 Arrange the "chips" in a single layer on a baking parchment- or foil-lined baking sheet. Brush with the melted butter. Bake for about 7 minutes, until lightly browned around the edges.

3 Meanwhile, in a blender or food processor, combine the ice cream, milk, chocolate syrup, malted drink powder, and vanilla extract. Process until well-blended but still thick. Divide among 8 small chilled glasses. Place 1 mini shake on each dessert plate, with several warm "chips" on the side. Serve at once.

INGREDIENTS

305g all-butter Madeira cake

3tbsp unsalted butter, melted

500ml (16fl oz) Tahitian Double Vanilla Ice Cream (page 12), Chocolate Custard Ice Cream (page 30), or store-bought vanilla or chocolate ice cream

240ml (8fl oz) milk, chilled

3tbsp Chocolate Syrup (page 179), or store-bought chocolate syrup

3tbsp malted drink powder

½tsp vanilla extract

Makes 8 120ml (4fl oz) servings

Ginger Beer Float

In this world of snazzy coffee drinks, it's easy to overlook something as old-fashioned as ginger beer, a sparkling ginger-flavoured soft drink containing Jamaican root ginger. When paired with home-made ice cream, it's hard to think of a more delectable combination.

Pour about 4tbsp of ginger beer into the bottoms of 4 tall, chilled glasses. Add a large scoop of ice cream to each, mashing with a spoon to form a thick liquid. Add a second scoop of ice cream. Fill the glasses with the remaining ginger beer and serve at once.

INGREDIENTS

750ml (1¼ pints) ginger beer

500ml (16fl oz) Tahitian Double Vanilla Ice Cream (page 12), or your favourite premium brand

Makes 4 large floats

VARIATIONS

Black Cow: Substitute cola for the ginger beer.

Ginger Ale Float: Substitute ginger ale for the ginger beer.

Vanilla Shake

For those who love vanilla, the simpler the better. Here's an old-fashioned shake that doesn't rock the boat.

In a blender or food processor, combine the ice cream, milk, and vanilla extract. Process until well-blended but still thick. Pour into tall, chilled glasses and serve at once.

INGREDIENTS

1 litre (2 pints) Tahitian Double Vanilla Ice Cream (page 12), or your favourite premium brand

360ml (12fl oz) milk, chilled

1tsp vanilla extract

Makes 2 large shakes

**Coffee Shake
(see Variation below)**

1 litre (2 pints) Coffee Ice Cream (page 32), or store-bought coffee ice cream

360ml (12fl oz) cold brewed coffee

1tbsp Kahlúa or 1tsp vanilla extract

Makes 2 large shakes

VARIATION

Coffee Shake: In a blender or food processor, combine the coffee ice cream, coffee, and Kahlúa or vanilla extract. Process until well-blended but still thick. Pour into tall, chilled glasses and serve at once.

Sauces, Toppings, & Pie Crusts

Bittersweet Fudge Sauce

240ml (8fl oz) double cream

2tbsp golden syrup

Pinch of salt

225g (8oz) plain dark chocolate, finely chopped

1tsp vanilla extract or 1tbsp Cognac, Kahlúa, or Grand Marnier

In a heavy medium saucepan, combine the cream, golden syrup, and salt. Bring to the boil over a medium heat, whisking frequently, until well-blended. Remove from the heat. Add the chocolate and whisk until melted and smooth. Let the sauce cool for 10–15 minutes. Stir in the vanilla extract and use at once, or refrigerate, covered, for up to 1 week. Serve warm or at room temperature.

Makes about 350ml (12fl oz)

Chocolate-Nut Sauce

85g (3oz) whole blanched almonds, or pecan or walnut pieces, or roasted peanuts

350g (12oz) plain dark chocolate, finely chopped

Pinch of salt

Preheat the oven to 180°C (350°F/Gas 4). If using peanuts, skip to the next step. Spread out the nuts in a small baking pan. Toast in the oven for 7–10 minutes, stirring once or twice, until lightly browned and fragrant. Transfer to a dish and let cool, then chop coarsely. Place a heatproof bowl over a pot of barely simmering water. Add the chocolate and cook over a low heat, stirring, until melted and smooth. Stir in the nuts and salt. Serve warm.

Makes about 350ml (12fl oz)

Chocolate Ganache

240ml (8fl oz) double cream

Pinch of salt

225g (8oz) plain dark chocolate, finely chopped

In a small saucepan, combine the cream and salt. Bring to the boil over a medium heat. Remove from the heat and add the chopped chocolate; stir until melted and smooth. Let cool until the sauce is fluid but not thin. If made in advance, refrigerate for up to 1 week. Reheat gently before serving.

Makes about 350ml (12fl oz)

Easy Chocolate Sauce

175g (6oz) sugar

4tbsp golden syrup

120ml (4fl oz) warm water

Pinch of salt

115g (4oz) plain dark chocolate, finely chopped

½tsp vanilla extract

In a medium saucepan, combine the sugar, golden syrup, 4tbsp of the warm water, and the salt. Bring to the boil over a medium-high heat. Reduce the heat to low and stir for 1 minute or until sugar dissolves. Remove from the heat and add the chocolate; stir until melted and smooth. Set aside for 10 minutes. Stir in the vanilla extract and the remaining 4tbsp warm water. Serve at once or cover and refrigerate for up to 1 week. Serve slightly warm.

Makes about 350ml (12fl oz)

Mocha Fudge Sauce

175g (6oz) plain chocolate chips

180ml (6fl oz) double cream

1tbsp instant coffee granules

Pinch of salt

4tbsp golden syrup

Place the chocolate chips in

a bowl and set aside. In a medium saucepan, combine the cream, coffee granules, and salt. Cook, stirring, until the coffee is dissolved and the liquid is barely simmering. Stir in the golden syrup and remove from the heat. Immediately pour the warm coffee cream over the chocolate chips. Let stand for 2 minutes, then whisk until melted and smooth. Use at once or let cool to room temperature, then cover and refrigerate for up to 1 week. To serve, reheat the sauce gently in the top of a double boiler or in the microwave.

Makes about 350ml (12fl oz)

Chocolate Whipped Cream

6tbsp unsweetened cocoa powder

85g (3oz) granulated sugar

240ml (8fl oz) double cream

Sift the cocoa powder and sugar through a fine sieve placed over a large bowl. Gradually whisk in the cream until blended. Cover and refrigerate for at least 30 minutes to dissolve the sugar and cocoa. Whisk with an electric mixer until soft peaks form. (This mixture whips up very quickly, so be careful not

to overbeat.) Use at once or cover and refrigerate for up to 2 hours.

Makes about 475ml (16fl oz)

Vanilla Toffee Sauce

175g (6oz) unsalted butter, cut into pieces

350g (12oz) dark brown sugar

180ml (6fl oz) double cream

Pinch of salt

1½tsp vanilla extract or 1½tbsp brandy

In a heavy medium saucepan, combine the butter, brown sugar, cream, and salt. Bring to the boil over a medium-high heat, stirring constantly with a wooden spoon. Remove from the heat and let cool for 10 minutes. Stir the vanilla extract into the warm toffee sauce. Serve at once, or refrigerate, covered, for up to 1 week. Reheat gently before serving.

Makes about 475ml (16fl oz)

Toffee Sauce

115g (4oz) unsalted butter, cut into pieces

225g (8oz) sugar

Pinch of salt

240ml (8fl oz) double cream, at room temperature

In a heavy 1-litre saucepan, melt the butter over a medium heat. Stir in the sugar and salt. Cook until the caramel turns a medium amber colour. (Don't

worry if the butter and sugar separate or become grainy at this point; they will come together later.) Remove the pan from the heat and slowly whisk in the cream. Let the sauce cool to room temperature, then cover and refrigerate. Serve chilled or at room temperature. If made more than a few hours in advance, transfer to a glass jar with a tight-fitting lid and refrigerate for up to 1 week.

Makes about 475ml (16fl oz)

Toffee Banana-Rum Sauce

75g (2½oz) brown sugar

75ml (2½fl oz) dark rum, such as Myers's

60g (2oz) unsalted butter, cut into pieces

⅛tsp ground cinnamon

⅛tsp freshly-grated nutmeg

60ml (2fl oz) double cream

3 large firm but ripe bananas

Combine the brown sugar and rum in a heavy nonreactive 1-litre saucepan. Cook over a medium-high heat, stirring often, for 4–5 minutes, or until the sugar melts, large bubbles appear on the surface, and the mixture has thickened. Reduce the heat to medium and add the butter. Stir frequently, until the butter has melted. Stir in the cinnamon and nutmeg.

Carefully stir in the cream, 1tbsp at a time. Cut the bananas crossways into ½cm (¼in) thick slices and add them to the sauce, stirring gently to coat. Reduce heat to low and simmer until the bananas are slightly cooked but hold their shape. Remove the sauce from the heat and let cool for 5–10 minutes before spooning over each serving.

Makes about 475ml (16fl oz)

Maple-Bathed Walnuts

115g (4oz) walnut pieces
4tbsp maple syrup
4tbsp golden syrup

Preheat the oven to 180°C (350°F/Gas 4). Spread out the walnuts evenly in a baking pan. Toast in the oven for 8–10 minutes, stirring once or twice, until lightly browned and fragrant. Transfer to a dish and set aside to cool. In a medium bowl, combine the toasted walnuts, maple syrup, and golden syrup. Stir until the nuts are well coated. Store in a covered jar in the refrigerator.

Makes about 350g (12oz)

Shortcrust Pastry Shell

115g (4oz) plain flour
2tbsp sugar
⅛tsp salt
115g (4oz) cold unsalted butter, cut into 8 pieces

Preheat the oven to 190°C (375°F/Gas 5). Lightly coat a 23cm (9in) tart tin with a removable bottom with cooking spray. Set the tart tin on a baking sheet. In a food processor, combine the flour, sugar, and salt. Process briefly to blend. Add the butter and pulse until the mixture forms coarse crumbs and begins to hold together. Turn out the dough and knead a few times until smooth. Press the dough evenly onto the bottom and up the sides of the tart tin. Bake for 15–18 minutes, until the crust is light golden. Transfer the tart tin to a wire rack and cool completely. If you are preparing a filling that requires baking, leave the crust in the tin and proceed with the recipe. Otherwise, gently remove the sides of the tin, leaving the shell on the metal bottom.

Makes 1 (9-inch) tart shell

Digestive Biscuit Crumb Crust

250g (9oz) digestive biscuit crumbs
2tbsp sugar
85g (3oz) unsalted butter, melted

Preheat the oven to 160°C (325°F/Gas 3). In a medium bowl, mix together the cookie crumbs and sugar until well-blended. Add the butter, stirring to moisten all of the crumbs. Press the mixture evenly over the bottom and up the sides of a 23cm (9in) pie tin, building the crumbs up slightly to form a small ridge above the rim of the tin. Bake the pie crust for 10 minutes. Let cool completely, then chill the crust in the freezer for at least 15 minutes before filling it with ice cream.

Makes 1 23cm (9in) pie crust

Ginger Nut Crumb Crust

250g (9oz) ginger nut cookie crumbs
2tbsp sugar
85g (3oz) unsalted butter, melted

Preheat the oven to 160°C (325°F/Gas 3). In a medium bowl, mix together the cookie crumbs and sugar until well-blended. Add the butter, stirring to moisten all of the crumbs. Press the mixture evenly over the bottom and up the sides of a 23cm (9in) pie tin, building the crumbs up slightly to form a small ridge above the rim of the tin. Bake the ginger nut crumb crust for 10 minutes. Let cool completely, then chill the crust in the freezer for at least 15 minutes before filling it with ice cream.

Makes 1 23cm (9in) pie crust

Chocolate Crumb Crust

350g (12oz) chocolate cookie crumbs
2tbsp sugar
85g (3oz) unsalted butter, melted

Preheat the oven to 160°C (325°F/Gas 3). In a medium bowl, mix together the cookie crumbs and sugar until well-blended. Add the butter, stirring to moisten all of the crumbs. Press the mixture over the bottom and up the sides of a 23cm (9in) pie tin, building the crumbs up slightly to form a small ridge above the rim. Bake for 10 minutes. Cool completely, then chill the crust in the freezer for 15 minutes before filling it with ice cream.

Makes 1 23cm (9in) pie crust

Chocolate Curls

1 large bar or piece (at least 115g or 4oz) white, milk, or plain chocolate, at warm room temperature

Use kitchen paper to hold the chocolate by its edge so the heat from your fingers doesn't melt it. Working over a baking sheet lined with baking parchment, use a swivel-bladed vegetable peeler to gently press against the edges of the chocolate bar and "peel" away curls. Let the curls fall onto the baking parchment. Avoid touching the chocolate, as the heat from your hands could be enough to melt the curls. Refrigerate or freeze the baking sheet for 15 minutes, or until the chocolate curls are firm to the touch. Cover with cling film or, working quickly, use a metal spatula to carefully transfer the curls to an airtight container. Refrigerate or freeze until needed. To serve, use a metal spatula to lift the cold chocolate curls from the baking parchment and place them on the ice cream.

Makes enough to garnish 4–6 servings

Brandied Fruit Sauce

1 orange
1 lemon
2 Granny Smith or other tart green apples, peeled, deseeded, and chopped
180ml (6fl oz) apple juice
100g (3½oz) chopped stoned dates
85g (3oz) sultanas
75ml (2½fl oz) bourbon whiskey, brandy, or dark rum
4tbsp dried currants
4tbsp finely chopped candied angelica, pineapple, or lemon peel
60g (2oz) brown sugar
4tbsp water
2tbsp cider vinegar
30g (1oz) unsalted butter
½tsp ground cinnamon
⅛tsp grated nutmeg
⅛tsp ground cardamom

Grate the rind from half the orange and half the lemon. Squeeze out the juice from both whole fruits. Combine the rind and juice with all of the other ingredients in a nonreactive large saucepan. Bring to the boil, partially cover, and cook over a medium heat, stirring occasionally, for 15–20 minutes, or until the apples are tender and the sauce has thickened. Let cool; then cover and refrigerate.

Makes about 475ml (16fl oz)

WOLVERHAMPTON LIBRARIES

Frozen dessert glossary

The vast variety of frozen desserts is one of the pleasures of home-made. In this book, whether a frozen dessert is technically an ice cream, a frozen custard, or a light ice cream is somewhat arbitrary, though the designation does give you an idea of the fat content and richness. Here are how the terms are defined:

Ice Cream: Generally designated by its higher concentration of butterfat (i.e., cream), ice cream comes in two varieties: "Philadelphia-style" ice creams do not contain eggs; custard-style ice creams, which most resemble commercially-made super-premium brands, are made from a cooked egg-custard base.

Frozen Custard: Ice cream made with an egg yolk-custard base. Many frozen custards are simply called "ice cream."

Gelato: Synonymous with Italian ice cream, gelato traditionally contains only a small amount of butterfat. Commercially-made gelato has less air churned into it than ice cream, giving it a denser texture. Gelato may or may not contain eggs.

Light Ice Cream: Containing milk products other than double cream—usually single cream—light ice cream is richer than ice milk, but less rich than ice cream.

Ice Milk: Ice milk contains no cream, which makes it lower in fat. It is often served softer than ice cream, as it has a tendency to become icy when frozen solid. Ice milks are best eaten within a day or two.

Sherbet: An eggless ice mixture of fruit and milk or cream, churned along with sugar and other flavourings.

Sorbet: An ice generally made without dairy products. It is usually fruit-based, but chocolate and coffee are also popular flavours.

Ice (sometimes called *Italian Ice*): The American version of granita. Most popular in the Northeastern United States, ices are often served in paper cups. Primarily made from syrups or other liquids, or sometimes fruit, its texture is smoother than a Snow Cone but not as granular as a granita.

Granita: An Italian ice that derives its fluffy, granular texture from repeated stirring and scraping as it freezes.

Frozen Yoghurt: Very similar to ice cream in texture, frozen yoghurt is far lower in calories. Yoghurt has a rich, slightly acidic taste that pairs particularly well with fruit.

Frozen Soya Milk: Offering a healthful alternative for people with special dietary needs, frozen soya milk provides a very satisfactory substitute for cow's milk when combined with flavourings.

Index

Page numbers in *italics* refer to photographs

Author's Acknowledgements

A heartfelt month of sundaes go to fellow food professionals who generously contributed their recipe development and testing skills to this book: Karen Baxter, John Carroll, Linda Gollober, Beth Hensperger, Joyce Jue, Rosemary Mark, Michelle Schmidt, and Barbara Shenson.

Sweet recognition also goes to "international correspondents" Gary Doherty, David Pantalena, and Gabrielle Saylor who promptly answered all of my late-night emails with wisdom and good humor.

A double-dip thank you to Rachel Litner, Mary Rodgers, Ilona Gollinger and Cuisinart, and to Lello Appliances for providing ice cream machines for testing and photography.

Cherry-topped kudos to Susan Wyler, who once again condensed my ramblings into readable prose.

And to Nichole Morford at DK Publishing, a flurry of thanks for staying cool while making split decisions.